MW01681033

Nurturing Program
For Parents and Children Birth to Five Years™

Parent Handbook

Stephen J. Bavolek and Juliana Dellinger Bavolek, M.S.E.

Family Development Resources, Inc.

©1985, 1988 by Family Development Resources, Inc.

Published 1985 as Family Resource Handbook

Second Edition 1988

Printed in the United States of America

ISBN #0-934309-11-6

All rights reserved, including translation. No part of this book or other materials of the Nurturing Program for Parents and Children Birth to Five Years covered by the copyright hereon may be reproduced in any form of printing or by any other means, electronic or mechanical including, but not limited to, photocopying, audio-visual recording and transmission, and portrayal or duplication in any information storage and retrieval system.

Family Development Resources, Inc.
219 E. Madison Street
Eau Claire, WI 54703

Welcome Parents and Children

We're glad you have chosen to participate in the Nurturing Program. It's an exciting program, and we're confident that you and the other members of your family who participate will not only learn some new skills, but will also have fun.

Parenting children is not an easy task. As a parent, you probably already know that. Some families have an easier time of it than others, but we suspect all families, at various times, struggle a bit. The Nurturing Program is our attempt to make the struggles more and more infrequent for both you and your children. After all, what is a struggle for you is almost certain to be a struggle for your children.

We believe learning new skills, attitudes, and knowledge about nurturing ways to parent children is the way to make family problems less significant. But there's a catch to learning new behavior: You must be open to take risks and be willing to let go of old beliefs and practices. New knowledge and attitudes are ready to replace old ones, but only if you allow it to happen. Change is seldom easy; sometimes it's downright painful, but it can occur. It's up to you! The degree of commitment you make to learning will probably be equal to the degree of change you experience. You should realize, however, that the commitment you make to establishing nurturing parent/child ways of interacting is likely to have profound effects on future generations of children in your family. After all, we are what we experience.

To help you and your family in this adventure of learning, we would like to dedicate this book to you. It's our way of saying thank you for letting our ideas into your lives.

We wish you and your children a peaceful, nurturing life together.

Stephen J. Bavolek
Juliana Dellinger Bavolek

About the Authors

Stephen J. Bavolek, Ph.D., is a nationally recognized leader in the field of parent education and the prevention and treatment of child abuse and neglect. He has a professional background working with emotionally disturbed children and adolescents in schools and residential settings, and abused children and abusive parents in treatment programs. He completed a postdoctoral internship at the Kempe Center for the Prevention and Treatment of Child Abuse in Denver, Colorado, and was selected by Phi Delta Kappa as one of 75 young educators in the country who represent the best in educational leadership, research, and services. Dr. Bavolek has conducted extensive research in the prevention and treatment of child abuse and neglect. He is the author of *A Handbook for Understanding Child Abuse and Neglect*, a comprehensive examination of maltreatment to children, and the *Adult-Adolescent Parenting Inventory*, a valid measure designed to assess high risk parenting attitudes.

Juliana Dellinger Bavolek, M.S.E., is a parent-child training specialist. Ms. Bavolek's professional background includes intensive experience with preschool handicapped children and their families, both as a classroom teacher/home visitor and as a facilitator of support groups for parents of infants and toddlers with special needs. As a training specialist with the Portage Project Region V Home Start Training Center, Ms. Bavolek provided training and technical assistance to Headstart home visit staff in implementing services for culturally disadvantaged parents and their preschool children. Ms. Bavolek served as the Education/Handicap Services Coordinator for Headstart and Parent-Child Centers in a seven county area in Wisconsin, and continues to work as a consultant to special education programs in the public schools and to Headstart and Parent-Child Centers nationally.

Contents

1

The Nurturing Program for Parents and Children

Welcome to the Nurturing Program. As you probably already know, raising children is not an easy task. Being a parent requires dedication, sacrifice, skill, knowledge, love, and compassion. The hours are long, there are no paid vacations, and you must be on call 24 hours every day of the year to perform activities that range from changing diapers to comforting a frightened child. In our culture, the fascination toward becoming a mother or father is unequaled. At some time in their lives, almost all young girls and boys dream about the day that they will have children of their own. Surprisingly, the majority of us who do become parents do so with little or no formal training.

Learning to Become Parents

Did you ever wonder how adults learn to become parents? For the most part, young men and women learn about raising children through various informal means. Let's review some of the popular beliefs.

"Now, where did the diaper go?"

Parenting is Instinctual

An instinct is an inborn tendency to act in a certain manner. Some people believe that raising children is instinctual and that this ability is brought out when your first child is born. Supposedly, parents are then capable of providing the love, nurturing, skill, and compassion necessary to raise a healthy child.

Parenting is Learned

Not everyone supports the instinctual theory of parenting. Many believe that parenting is a learned behavior that starts very early in our lives. The way we learn how to become parents is a process that is called modeling. Modeling means that as parents, we use the same techniques for raising our children that our parents used on us when we were kids.

The expressions "like father-like son" or "like mother-like daughter" suggest that we will behave like our father, or mother because of the many experiences we had with them. Our parents had a certain style and philosophy about discipline, punishment, communication, chores, expectations, etc. Because we were brought up with their manner of parenting, we learned their techniques. Given similar situations, we will "model" their behaviors with our own children.

Parenting is learned through modeling.

Modeling the Behaviors of Others

Although the experiences we had with our parents probably account for the greater part of our parenting training, there are other factors which have influenced our style of child rearing. Our parenting abilities are influenced by the environment we grew up in, our parent's financial status, the culture or subculture our family was a part of, our ethnic heritage, our race, our religious beliefs, our birth order, and whether we are male or female.

Modeling Appropriate Behaviors

For many of us, the messages we received and the models we watched were mostly positive and gave us a good start in parenting our children. Although there were bad times, the majority of interactions with mom and dad were positive and left a good impression.

Modeling Abusive Behaviors

For a lot of us, however, the messages we received and the models we observed were frequently negative and resulted in learning inappropriate parenting behaviors.

Modeling can be negative.

Harsh and abusive parents, experiences, and environments leave in their wake a distorted view of what the roles of a child and a parent are all about. Their impact is observed in the countless number of abusive acts committed each year on children, spouses, and the elderly.

The Nurturing Program for Parents and Children

Our belief is that parenting is a learned behavior, and that old undesirable patterns of interactions between parents and children can be replaced with new, more desirable ones. The parenting and nurturing program that you and your family will be a part of is built around this premise.

Learning Appropriate Developmental Expectations

Part of our focus will be on increasing your knowledge of the developmental capabilities of children at various ages. Such knowledge will better prepare you to establish age-appropriate expectations for your children's behavior.

Children learn to do things at different ages.

You will learn how and when children can accomplish certain tasks, and the physical, social, and emotional skills necessary to complete the tasks.

You will also become aware of the negative impact inappropriate expectations have upon a developing self-concept.

You will not be alone in learning these skills. Because your entire family will be involved in the program, your children will be learning comparable skills. Activities in the children's program encourage the development of a positive self-concept by allowing children to master age-appropriate tasks.

Learning Appropriate Behavior Management Techniques

A major part of our focus will be on increasing your knowledge and ability to use appropriate behavior management techniques with your children. We base our training on the philosophy that hitting children for any reason is abusive.

Appropriate behavior management techniques.

During the program, we will discuss and role play various appropriate ways of disciplining and punishing your children that are immeasurably more effective than hitting.

Your children will also be learning identical forms of discipline and ways of being punished when they choose to violate the standards of appropriate behavior established by the group leaders. Our goal is to give you and your children experiences in appropriate types of discipline and punishment.

Increasing Self-Awareness

Raising healthy children takes more than sheer knowledge, that is, having the right expectations, or knowing appropriate ways of disciplining and punishing your children. Parenting children is also a deeply emotional experience that requires you, the parent, to maintain an awareness of your own needs.

Mother role/hostess role.

Not losing sight of your own social and emotional needs as an individual will help you in maintaining an identity of yourself outside of your role as a parent. Becoming aware of and being able to find ways to meet your needs, is a major focus of our program.

Activities will challenge you to understand who you are by identifying your personal strengths and weaknesses. Our experiences have told us that when parents become aware of themselves as individuals, they increase their ability to become healthy, loving, nurturing parents to their children.

In addition, your children will also be increasing their awareness of their own needs, feelings, strengths, weaknesses, likes, and dislikes through art, music, communication, and group activities. You and your children will be growing together through an awareness of your self needs.

Increasing Ability to be Empathic

In becoming a nurturing parent, you will utilize awareness of your feelings, your strengths, weaknesses, likes, and dislikes to become more aware of the feelings, strengths, weaknesses, likes, and dislikes of your children. It forms the cornerstone of our program.

Nurturing people have empathy.

Being empathic means you will be able to help your children grow up as healthy, independent, caring, empathic individuals. What more could any child ever ask of his parents.

Your children will also be increasing their ability to become empathically aware of the needs of others. Group activities will encourage children to share, play cooperatively, listen to the needs of others, and support a friend in time of need.

Learning new skills and knowledge is not always an easy task. But with a sincere effort, you and your family can begin to enjoy more satisfying and caring interactions.

WELCOME TO OUR PROGRAM!

2

Behavior Management

Helping Children Learn Appropriate Behaviors

Managing children's behavior is one of the most important responsibilities of a parent. Children need to learn right from wrong, which behaviors are acceptable and which behaviors are nonacceptable, in order to grow up as healthy and contributing members of a family and society. Parents need to be able to manage their children's behaviors in order to create a supportive and caring family for themselves as well as their children. To help children develop into healthy beings, parents use a variety of techniques and types of interactions to communicate—"I like or don't like you" and "I like or don't like what you are doing."

Some ways in which parents try to manage their children's behaviors are not appropriate. Abusive interactions between parents and children benefit neither parents nor children. Abusive interactions do not teach the children what is right and acceptable. Managing children's behaviors using nonabusive techniques is not an easy task for any parent. You will need to devote time and effort to master these techniques. Because of your effort, however, you and your family will be rewarded with a happier and more satisfying family life.

Let's start by describing what we mean by the terms behavior management, discipline, punishment and rewards .

What is Behavior Management?

Behavior management is a general term used to describe techniques parents use to help their children learn appropriate and desirable behaviors. Some examples of behavior management include praising desired behavior, ignoring undesirable behavior, modeling appropriate behavior, and punishing inappropriate behavior. These techniques are used by parents to teach children to obey rules; to meet parent expectations for safety, school performance, and cleanliness; and, to punish unacceptable behaviors. Whether you are aware of it or not, as a parent you are constantly using behavior management techniques.

Behavior management includes techniques used to establish guidelines for behavior which we call discipline; techniques used to reduce inappropriate behavior which we call punishment; and, techniques used to increase appropriate behavior which we call rewards.

What is Discipline?

Discipline is the rules, guidelines, and standards for acceptable behavior that parents establish for their children. Discipline forms boundaries within which children learn to act and behave in a socially acceptable manner. For example, discipline may include responsibilities children have at home, curfew imposed by a parent, family rules such as no hitting, or no throwing things, standards for cleanliness, and the consequences for not obeying the rules. The message parents send to children through discipline is "I care about you and will set limits and consequences to help you learn to manage your own behavior."

Discipline includes rules established by parents.

What is Punishment?

Punishment is a penalty administered by a parent to a child when the child has chosen to break one or more of the rules, guidelines, or standards for acceptable behavior that have been set by the parents. Appropriate types of punishment may include time-out, loss of privilege, or replacement of a broken object. A child who has purposefully broken a toy may have to sit in time-out for five minutes, or may lose the privilege of playing with other toys for a day. An older child may have to pay for or replace the broken toy.

Loss of privilege can be used as punishment.

What Are Rewards?

Rewards are given to a child by a parent when the child has obeyed the family rules or has behaved appropriately. Rewards can be intangible, like praise for being and doing, smiles, or pleasing others. Rewards can also be tangible like special privileges, allowances, or use of the telephone. The goal behind rewards is to let children know their behavior is appropriate and appreciated.

The Difference Between Punishment and Discipline

Like rewards, both punishment and discipline are forms of behavior management. However, there is a big difference between the two concepts. Discipline is the rules and expectations parents have for their children's behavior. Punishment is the actions taken by parents when rules or expectations have been purposefully broken.

Let's use an example to illustrate the difference. In sports, players have to follow certain rules or standards. Let's call these rules "discipline." The rules are necessary for the game to be played in the expected manner. When a rule is broken, the player or team is administered a penalty by the referee. The hockey player who picks a fight with another player receives a "punishment." Fighting is not allowed. The referee tells the player he has to sit in the penalty box for five minutes. At home when children fight, they too are given a penalty or punishment. Fighting at home is against family rules. The referee in this instance is the mother or father who tells the child he too has to sit for five minutes in the penalty box. At home, we call this penalty box *time-out*. However, for the punishment to have meaning, the rules must be clear, consistent, and fair.

At home, mother or father is the referee.

The Rules Must be Clear and Consistent

Without clear and consistent rules, there can be no just punishment. If the players didn't know the rules of the game, or if the rules of the game kept changing every week, it would be impossible for the players to know what is allowed and what isn't allowed. Without this knowledge, players who were punished would begin to feel angry and resentful toward the referee.

The same is true at home. Parents expect their children to behave in an acceptable manner. However, to behave in a manner in which the parents define as acceptable, children need to know the rules—what is acceptable and what is not acceptable.

"I didn't get in trouble for that yesterday!"

Of equal importance is the consistent presence of the rules. If the rules keep changing or disappearing, that is, what is acceptable on Tuesday is not acceptable on Saturday, the result will be feelings of confusion and eventually anger. Just like the hockey player, children too will become angry with parents and begin to feel the rules and the punishment are unfair.

The Rules Must be Fair

Rules established for children by parents must be fair. Remember, the intent of the rules is to let the children know what they can and can't do. Rules are not intended to inhibit the overall positive growth of the child. Rules that are too strict prevent the learning of independence, autonomy, and responsibility—the very things you want your children to learn. When children feel the rules you establish are too strict, you can discuss the issue with them and attempt to resolve the differences of opinion. When children feel the rules are too strict, and are not allowed an opportunity to discuss the rules, they may feel both the rules and the punishment are unfair.

Discuss rules, attempt to resolve differences.

Punishment Must be Immediate, Consistently Enforced, and Non-Abusive

When children know the rules, violation of the rules must be dealt with in an immediate, consistent, and non-abusive manner. There are three key factors that will ensure just and effective punishment:

1. The time between the behavior and the punishment.
2. The consistency of enforcing the rules.
3. The fair, nonabusive manner in which the punishment is administered.

Time

To be most effective, the punishment has to be given immediately following the inappropriate behavior. A short time span helps children understand the relationship between the inappropriate behavior and the punishment. It is not good to have a lot of time elapse between the inappropriate behavior and the punishment because children may become confused and may not remember why they are being punished.

Punishment is administered immediately.

Consistency

To reduce the number of times children misbehave, the punishment has to be administered every time the misbehavior occurs. If the punishment is only occasionally administered, children will experience confusion, may learn how to be manipulative, and will often feel the punishment is unjust. Being consistent in the administration of nonabusive punishment every time the misbehavior occurs is a key ingredient to the overall success of helping children learn what is acceptable and what is not acceptable.

Nonabusive Punishment

How the punishment is applied is just as important as the type of punishment used. A key to punishment is to create a home environment with clear and consistent consequences for inappropriate behavior. When such an atmosphere exists, when rules or standards are violated, the punishment is a logical consequence to the behavior and can be viewed by all as fair. Hitting, yelling, threatening, belittling children are practices we feel are abusive. They teach children that they are not good rather than their behavior is unacceptable.

Inappropriate behavior management is abusive.

Throughout the program, we will be discussing both appropriate and inappropriate ways parents interact with their children. Our goal is to help you develop appropriate, nonabusive behavior management skills so you can successfully use them in helping your children learn acceptable behaviors. The systematic use of nonabusive behavior management techniques will ultimately lead to happier, more satisfying interactions between you and your children.

3

Family Rules

Family rules are the single most important part of helping children learn right from wrong. They teach children what is acceptable behavior to mom and dad and what is not. Family rules also allow children to please their parents by trying hard to do the right things. Boys and girls love being praised for being and doing. Children begin to understand the idea of family rules around two years of age and enjoy contributing in developing the rules. At an early age, children realize that expectations of them are equal to the expectations of mom, dad, and other family members.

Tentative List of Family Rules

Brainstorm a list of four or five possible family rules.

What To Do:	What Not To Do:
1.	1.
2.	2.
3.	3.
4.	4.
5.	5.

Rules For The ________________ Family

What To Do:	What Not To Do:
1.	1.
2.	2.
3.	3.
4.	4.
5.	5.

4

Needs and Payoffs for Adults and Children

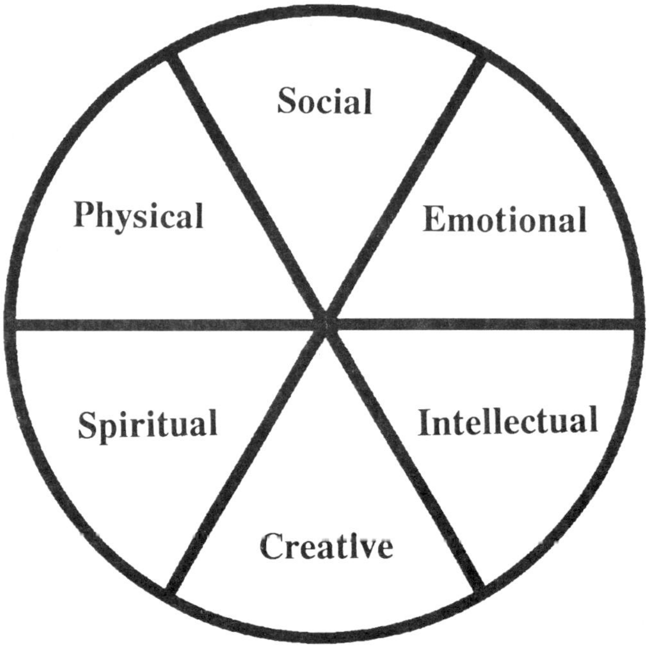

Social Needs
The need for friendship, for companionship.

Emotional Needs
The need for love, for praise, for feeling worthwhile.

Intellectual Needs
The need for intellectual stimulation, for thinking new thoughts, for reading challenging books, for learning something new.

Physical Needs
The need for sleep, for food, for exercise.

Creative Needs
The need to make something, to dance, to write a poem, to create something.

Spiritual Needs
The need to know that we are part of something bigger than ourselves and that we can increase our awareness of and sensitivity to it.

Behavior Payoffs

A payoff is something we receive when we get one or more of our needs met. Payoffs can either be good or bad. A good payoff is something we get that we want. We call good payoffs rewards. A bad payoff is something we get that we don't want. Bad payoffs are called consequences.

Let's look at an example. Suppose a man wants to lose some weight. His goal is to drop 30 pounds. He begins to diet by eating low caloric foods, staying away from snacks between meals, and exercising daily. Within two months, he has lost the 30 pounds. He soon learns that the payoffs or rewards for dieting are not only the loss of weight, but also a healthier, more attractive appearance, a longer life span, and a more active social life. Unfortunately, losing 30 pounds has made his clothes way too big on him. He now has to purchase new clothes several sizes smaller. Since he hadn't planned on spending money for new clothes, the bad payoff or consequence for dieting is spending money to buy new clothes. As a general rule, however, behavior will continue as long as the rewards outnumber the consequences.

"Boy, do I ever look and feel good!!"

In the above example, the man will continue to watch his weight and stick to his diet because the rewards of being slimmer outnumber the consequence of spending money to purchase new clothes.

Payoffs and Self-Esteem/Self-Concept

The way we feel about ourselves influences the way we get our needs met and the payoffs we receive. People who feel lousy about themselves generally do things to keep themselves feeling lousy. Feeling lousy is their payoff. The same is true with people who feel good about themselves. They do things to help themselves feel good. Feeling good is their payoff.

Positive or negative self-esteem and self-concept lead to appropriate or inappropriate behaviors which lead to positive or negative payoffs.

As you can see, how we think and feel about ourselves affects our behavior—which produces payoffs—which reinforces our thoughts and feelings about ourselves.

Think and feel positive!

Needs and Payoffs

Complete the following:

1. One need that I have, which is currently not being met, is ______________________________

   ____

2. One way I block getting my need for ____ met,

   is by ____ .

3. What are some good payoffs (rewards) and bad payoffs (consequences) I get from blocking my need?

   Rewards:

   a.

   b.

   c.

   d.

   Consequences:

   a.

   b.

   c.

   d.

4. Brainstorm ways to get the need met.

   a.

   b.

   c.

   d.

5

Spoiling Your Children

A spoiled child is a boy or girl who has learned to be defiant, demanding, and manipulative. Spoiled children do not respond well to limits placed on their behavior by their parents. They generally have a hard time waiting for things they want and will often respond with temper tantrums, hitting, breaking, or throwing things when told "no." It is important to recognize that children approximately one year and younger are never considered to be "spoiled." The developmental stage of infancy requires babies to demand their needs to be met. As they grow older, their needs become less demanding.

How Do Children Become Spoiled?

Spoiling children is not an easy task. It takes a lot of time, effort, and attentiveness on the part of a parent to spoil a child. Spoiling children requires a parent to perform the following behaviors:

- Do everything for a child so he does nothing for himself.
- Anticipate a child's request so he never has to ask for anything.
- Spend all your waking hours together.
- Prohibit any type of short separation from the child; even having a babysitter.
- Only pick a child up when he cries.
- Be inconsistent in the limits and rules you set down so a child never knows what to expect.
- Blame the child for being demanding and demonstrate anger toward him.

"Where did we go wrong?"

If you follow the above steps, you are guaranteed to have a spoiled child.

Myths and Facts About Spoiling Children

Myth: You will spoil your child by picking him up when he cries.

"Should we or shouldn't we?"

Fact: If the only time you hold your child is when he cries, the child soon learns he has to cry to be held. Picking him up only when he cries is a good way to spoil a child. Make sure you spend twice as much time holding your child when he's not crying. The child will at least learn he doesn't have to cry to be held.

Myth: Children who throw temper tantrums are spoiled.

Children express frustration through tantrums.

Fact: Temper tantrums are a way a young child expresses his frustration towards a situation or person. Young children are essentially very needy people; they want what they want now, not later. Setting reasonable limits helps children develop patience and delays in their need for gratification. Expect a few temper tantrums along the way and don't become too alarmed. Make sure you read the information on ignoring as a way of helping children learn other ways of expressing frustration.

Myth: A spoiled child is one who has not been spanked.

Fact: Spanking a child never prevented one from becoming spoiled. The absence of reasonable limits and consequences for inappropriate behavior contributes to spoiling a child, not the absence of spanking. Spanking is a type of hitting; hitting is a type of hurting touch; hurting touch is a type of abuse. A nurturing parent uses other, more effective, means of discipline and punishment than hitting.

Myth: A young child is incapable of doing anything for himself.

Children like doing things themselves.

Fact: Children can learn very early in life to participate in getting their own needs met. They can help in getting dressed, wiping their mouths after eating, feeding themselves, and brushing their teeth. Children enjoy doing things for themselves because they feel more powerful and more in control of their environment.

Myth: If my child is spoiled, to cure him I have to become harsh and mean.

Redirect a demanding child.

Fact: If you find you have spoiled your child, here are some suggestions:

- If your child is too demanding, when he wants to be picked up, explain that you have work to do and will hold him in a little while. Try redirecting him to a new activity.
- If your child wakes up once, or several times during the night — not only wanting your company, but also wanting to be entertained — he has to learn that there is nothing to be gained by waking and crying. It might mean letting the child cry 15 to 20 minutes the first few times without touching, talking, or even letting the child see you. Soon the crying will subside, although it may seem like forever.
- If your child has difficulty separating from you, try brief periods of being apart. You might first try inviting a babysitter over while you remain in the house so the child gets to feel comfortable with someone else. Then gradually go away for 5, 15, 25 minutes reassuring and praising the child when you return. Soon he will feel more secure and confident that you are not apt to abandon him.

Encourage Healthy Child Behaviors

No child is ever born spoiled. Becoming spoiled is a learned behavior like being afraid of the dark or not liking to eat certain foods. Children learn to be spoiled from the people who serve as their primary caregivers.

- Help your child by helping yourself learn new, nurturing parenting attitudes and child rearing practices.
- Pay attention to the needs of your child without overdoing it.
- Promote independence by encouraging your child to do things for himself.
- Model for your child the proper way to handle disappointment, frustration, and sadness so he can act more appropriately.

Promote independence.

Learn new, nurturing attitudes.

Model appropriate behaviors for your child.

The payoffs for encouraging healthy behavior in children last a lifetime!

6

Personal Power

Personal power is the emotional capability we have to influence conditions in our lives which helps us to meet our needs. Personal power is not how physically strong we are, but how emotionally strong we are. We can use our personal power in a positive or negative, destructive way.

Positive Personal Power

The use of our personal power in a positive sense means that we do things to meet our needs that build and strengthen our positive self-esteem and self-concept.

"I feel good about myself!"

As nurturing parents, we use our personal power to help build a positive sense of self in our children. In turn, we want our children to use their own personal power to meet their own needs in a positive way. People who use their personal power in a positive way generally feel good about themselves as men and women.

Negative Personal Power

Some people use their personal power in a negative way. That is, the things they do to get their needs met are destructive. Alcohol and drug dependency, fighting, stealing, cheating, or hitting are all ways people can use their personal power in a negative way.

People who use their personal power in a negative way generally feel bad about themselves as men and women. Our goal is to help people use their personal power in a positive way to reinforce positive self-concept and positive self-esteem.

To Develop a Sense of Personal Power in Yourself:

- Take ownership of your feelings.
- Take responsibility for your own behavior.
- Make decisions to problems that will increase your sense of self-worth.
- Communicate using I statements.
- Praise yourself for being and doing.
- Follow through with commitments.
- Be aware of the needs and feelings of others.

Develop a positive personal power in yourself.

To Develop a Sense of Personal Power in Your Children:

- Treat children with respect and dignity.
- Praise your children for being and doing.
- Give children opportunities for success.
- Encourage your children to take responsibility for their feelings.
- Provide your children with choices and consequences.
- Listen and talk to your children.
- Respect your child's body.
- Be nurturing and consistent in helping children learn appropriate behaviors.

Children need to develop personal power also.

Control

Control is the use of your personal power to manage, dictate, and steer your own behavior— or another person's behavior and needs— for self gain.

Positive Control

Controlling another person's behavior is necessary when that person is unable to meet their own basic needs. Infants, elderly, disabled, mentally ill, and bedridden patients all require help in meeting their basic needs. In these instances, controlling a major part of a person's life is positive and appropriate.

Controlling an infant's behavior is OK.

Negative Control

Controlling another person's life when that person has the capability of managing his/her own behavior, or meeting his/her own needs is an inappropriate use of control. Children who can take responsibility for their own behavior, but are not allowed to, are being controlled in a negative way. These negative feelings will only lead to rebellion, inadequate feelings of self, and extreme forms of dependency.

7

Praising a Child's Behavior

Praise is a word, gesture, facial expression, or phrase that encourages children to feel pride and joy. Praise is a way of giving children positive feedback to increase their sense of worth, competence, and confidence.

When to Praise

In praising children, you are pointing out the worth of their abilities, traits, or achievements. When your child tries hard to do something, even if he doesn't finish, praise the effort. When your daughter brings home a completed project, praise the work. When your child looks good, tell him or her. When children do things that are pleasing, let them know. Praise them.

"You did a nice job dressing yourself."

Inappropriate Praise

There is such a thing as inappropriate praise. Inappropriate praise occurs when parents make evaluative statements regarding children's personalities, or when the praise is followed by a negative statement.

Evaluative statements about a child's personality may make him or her uneasy because the statements imply the parents are sitting in judgment. The child may be a great kid today only because he or she is doing something that pleases mom or dad. Tomorrow, if mom and dad aren't pleased, the child may not be considered "great."

Another form of inappropriate praise occurs when a critical statement accompanies a praise statement. Parents who use this type of communication send the child double messages. "You are a great kid, but...," or "I like what you did, however...." These messages change the focus of the communication from positive to negative and are not considered praise.

Praise with a critical statement isn't effective.

Praise should be clear, positive messages which focus on the child's behavior that is pleasing and accepting.

Promoting Self-Praise in Children

Self-praise is a way children can learn the habit of praising themselves to boost their self-image. To help a child learn self-praise, parents need to describe how good an action must have made the child feel. Imagine yourself in the child's shoes and describe the feeling. By promoting self-praise, children develop an internal evaluation process that is both realistic and genuine.

Modeling Self-Praise

To encourage children to use self-praise, parents should model the behavior for them. Praise yourself in the presence of your children whenever you do something well, or whenever you feel proud of some effort. Modeling self-praise is an effective teaching procedure because children learn best by imitation.

Children learn praise through imitation.

Go ahead – toot your own horn!

How to Praise

1. Focus your attention on the child and the situation. Praise deserves your undivided attention.

2. Move close to the child. It feels good to be praised by someone close to you.

3. Make eye contact with the child on the child's level. For instance, stoop down to make eye contact with a two-year old – this makes it all the more special.

4. Look pleasant – everyone likes to see a happy face.

5. Describe what you see. "I see two children playing together," or "Boy, you sure made a good effort in trying to button your shirt."

6. Share your pleasure. "That's really nice to see," or "I am glad you tried buttoning."

7. Often a hug or a soft touch makes the message a lot stronger. It's nice to be touched while being praised, however, it's not necessary.

8. Remember – focus on the behavior. Love is unconditional and includes the whole child; praise is conditional and involves specific behaviors you want to see more of.

9. Praise anytime – there is no such thing as too much praise.

Praise encourages feelings of pride and joy.

8

Red, White, and Bruises

The Ancient Practice of Hitting

For as long as anyone cares to remember, hitting has been used by parents and other adults as a way of communicating their anger with children and their behaviors. Some say hitting children actually began thousands of years ago when cave people lived on the earth. Our image of cave parents running around with clubs hitting each other and their children on the head might be fairly accurate. Verbal language as a means of communication was slow in developing. Hitting was a way a cave mother said to her cave son, "I am not pleased with you, or what you did, or failed to do."

Although parents today generally don't use clubs, the practice of hitting children is unfortunately still widely used. The most widely used type of hitting today is spanking.

There are two common reasons why parents spank children: to educate and to punish.

Spanking to Educate

Many parents use spanking to try to teach their children right from wrong. Teaching children right from wrong is important for two primary reasons: personal safety and obedience to rules.

Personal safety is an important concept to teach children to prevent physical injury. Children who play in the street run the risk of being hit by a car. Children who play with matches increase their chances of burning themselves. Playing with electric sockets may cause children to be badly injured. Since parents don't want to see these things happen to their children, a punishment is usually administered. Children who run into the street are usually dragged back to the curb where they receive a yelling usually accompanied by a spanking. Children caught playing with matches or placing objects into electrical outlets may have their hands slapped. In these instances, spanking and hitting are used by parents and are logical consequences in teaching children about personal safety.

"I told you never to run into the street!"

Spanking as a Logical Consequence

Parents also use spanking as a way of teaching children obedience to family rules and social laws. Lying, cheating, and stealing are some examples of behaviors that are considered inappropriate and unacceptable. Children caught lying, stealing, or cheating may be severely spanked. Spanking as a logical consequence and educational tool has severe limitations in teaching children the desired behaviors. Spanking never teaches what is the right thing to do—it only punishes what is wrong.

Parents spank to try to teach obedience.

Spanking to Punish

Closely related to the practice of spanking children for educational purposes is the concept that children ought to be spanked as a punishment. Children who break rules, for example, deliberately throwing toys, are spanked because throwing toys is not permitted. Children who fight with their brothers and sisters may be spanked because fighting is not allowed.

Punishment is a necessary part of behavior management and should be used. However, hitting whether it is used as a punishment or for educational purposes, is not the best way to help children grow up healthy. The use of spanking often leaves a negative rather than positive impact on children.

Why Shouldn't I Hit My Child?

Hitting teaches something more than obeying rules and being careful. Hitting also teaches children fear, poor self-concept, revenge, and permission to hit those you love.

Fear

Hitting, even the threat of hitting, often teaches children fear. Children who learn to fear their parents often learn to fear other adults as well. Just the sheer difference in physical size between parents and children can be frightening. When parents threaten or use their physical superiority as a form of punishment, young children realize that there is no way they could ever win. Their safety is literally at the mercy of the angry parent.

"Daddy, you're scaring me!"

Poor Self-Concept

The self-concept of children develops in the manner in which the children are treated in their environment. Children who are constantly threatened or hit learn that they are not worthy people, are not loved, and are not wanted. Nobody ever feels good about himself after being hit. The more frequent the hitting, the more constant the feelings of inadequacy.

Revenge

Children who have been repeatedly hit want to seek revenge. Getting back is a common result of spanking. Young children who can't hit back may seek to get revenge in other ways. Breaking something that belongs to the parents, writing on the walls, or stealing are some ways children can "get back at" the person who is hitting. The idea of learning the appropriate behavior, or of being good, takes a back seat to feelings of revenge.

Stealing money is a form of revenge.

Permission to Hit Those You Love

Parents who hit children risk teaching children that hitting those you love is okay. In this way, children learn that hitting is permissible and acceptable. Statements like "Mommy loves you and is doing this for your own good," or "Daddy loves you very much and this is going to hurt me more than it will hurt you," only tend to confuse children and send double messages. Such confusion is carried over years later when children who were constantly spanked become parents and use the same practice on their children. We know that child abuse is often passed on from parents to children like a family heirloom.

Spanking hurts and is abusive!

Myths and Facts About the Value of Spanking

Myth: Children who aren't spanked become spoiled.

Spanking doesn't cure spoiled children.

Fact: Spoiled children are those who constantly want their own way, choose not to listen to parents, and are unaware of the needs of others. Although such behaviors are learned, they are not the result of not spanking. Such behaviors result from inconsistent parenting, failure to provide necessary structure, and neglect of children's needs. Spanking children to prevent them from becoming spoiled is only a myth. Being sensitive to the needs of children in a consistent, loving, nurturing way is the best means available to prevent children from becoming spoiled.

Myth: Only spank children when you are not angry.

"I'm not angry."

Fact: Such a statement is made to prevent parents from becoming too severe with their spanking. Some parents can't control their anger and feel that once they begin hitting their children, they won't be able to stop. The thought here is if children deserve to be punished, wait until you have calmed down before you spank. But, if you are not angry and have calmed down, why spank at all? You are in control. Talk to your children and let them know you are angry. Then use other forms of punishment you are learning in this program that are much more effective – such as time-out, or loss of privilege. You will feel better about the punishment and so will your children. What's more, managing their behavior will become a lot easier.

Myth: An occasional spanking is good for children.

Spanking or hitting doesn't feel good.

Fact: The word good indicates something beneficial is happening to the children. The truth is that an occasional spanking cannot help children learn behaviors parents feel are desirable. Hitting someone else, or being hit occasionally or frequently, never feels good and has no long-term value.

Myth: Spanking your children is the only way to let them know you're angry.

Hitting children is a poor way to relieve stress.

Fact: Parents often relieve their stress and frustration by hitting their children when they are angry with them. Although letting off steam is good for the parent, there is no value in the spanking for the children.

Myth: Infants need to be spanked because they can't understand the language.

A firm NO is better than spanking.

Fact: Hitting an infant is always a dangerous practice. The physical development of a young infant is too fragile to withstand any force. Because infants can't communicate verbally doesn't mean they can't learn. Infants learn from the touch, facial expressions, and tone of voice of the parents. A firm "no" spoken to an infant who is about to reach for a valued object is better than slapping the infant's hands. The "no" communicates your dislike of the behavior; the slap communicates your dislike of the infant.

Myth: Children deserve to be spanked.

Fact: Nobody ever deserves to be hit. The skills you are learning in this program will help you replace spanking with more beneficial and more pleasant ways of managing the behaviors of your children.

Goodbye spanking!

9

Baby Proofing Your House

Baby proofing is a term describing the actions parents take to make the living conditions of a house safe for a child.

Why Baby Proof?

Children, especially young toddlers, love to explore. Touching, pulling, grabbing, and eating are just a few of the ways young children explore their environment. Since toddlers are generally too young to know what is safe to play with and what is potentially dangerous, parents baby proof a house to protect children from becoming hurt, or in some instances, even killed.

Baby proofing prevents dangerous situations.

Parents also baby proof their house to enhance the positive interactions they have with their children. A house where dangerous objects are out of reach is a house where parents aren't constantly saying no.

Is Your House Baby Proofed?

You probably wonder at times whether your house is safe enough for your toddler to play in without a high risk for injury. There are two things you can do to see if your house is safe for toddlers:

1. Get down on your hands and knees and view the world as a toddler. What you can pull, grab, bite, so can your child. Move tempting and dangerous objects out of reach.
2. Watch your child as he explores his environment. Walk with your child through the house and notice what he notices. Can he reach that shelf? Can he push that button? Can he climb that chair? You'll soon find out by watching him. If he can reach objects he shouldn't, it's time to better baby proof your house.

View your house as your toddler sees it.

Once Baby Proofed, Always Baby Proofed?

Right? Wrong! Babies grow along with their ability to reach for objects, climb on furniture, open drawers, and walk up and down stairs. You will continually need to modify your house as your child continues to grow. The good news is that as your child grows older, he's also learning what is safe and what isn't.

As a child grows, so grows his reach.

Safety Checklist

The following safety checklist is designed to ensure your house is safe enough for your toddler to play in with only minimal risk of injury. Take some time now to go over this checklist, room by room, to make your house safe for your child. Make it a habit to recheck your house at least once a month.

All Rooms

To Do	Action	Done
( )	1. Put electric outlet covers on all unused outlets.	( )
( )	2. Put a gate across all stairways, top and bottom, until child can handle stairs.	( )
( )	3. Remove or pad sharp corners on furniture and appliances.	( )
( )	4. Remove throw rugs on tiled floors.	( )
( )	5. Use non-skid floor wax on wood, tile, or linoleum floors.	( )
( )	6. Keep all plants out of baby's reach.	( )

Kitchen

To Do	Action	Done
( )	1. Put all cleaning supplies on a top shelf out of children's reach.	( )
( )	2. Install safety locks on all kitchen cabinets below waist level. You may want to keep one cabinet with pots, pans, and unbreakable bowls unlocked for child's exploration.	( )
( )	3. Turn pot handles toward back of stove when cooking.	( )
( )	4. Take knobs off of gas ranges when not in use.	( )
( )	5. Have a secure cover for the garbage can.	( )
( )	6. Install safety locks on kitchen drawers with knives and other sharp utensils.	( )
( )	7. Keep all breakable bowls out of the cabinets with the pots and pans.	( )
( )	8. Remove throw rugs from kitchen floors.	( )
( )	9. Make sure highchairs are stable and have safety straps.	( )
( )	10. Remove tablecloth to prevent toddlers from pulling it off.	( )
( )	11. Keep items in use such as glasses, jars, bowls, utensils, etc. well back on the kitchen counter.	( )
( )	12. Remove pet food bowls to an area inaccessible to your baby.	( )

Bathroom

To Do	Action	Done
( )	1. Store all electrical appliances such as hair dryers, curling irons, electric toothbrushes in the bathroom cabinet or closet.	( )
( )	2. Put safety locks on all bathroom cabinets.	( )
( )	3. Remove all electrical appliances near water.	( )
( )	4. Place a non-skid bath mat on the bottom of tub.	( )
( )	5. Buy a rubber safety cover for the bathtub water faucets and spout to prevent accidental head injuries and scalding.	( )
( )	6. Keep all medicine in a locked medicine cabinet.	( )

Living Room

To Do	Action	Done
( )	1. Secure lamps and other freestanding objects.	( )
( )	2. Fence off fireplaces, wood stoves, space heaters, radiators, and heating grates.	( )
( )	3. Remove all breakable knickknacks and ashtrays.	( )
( )	4. Lock all gun cabinets.	( )
( )	5. Attach electrical lamp cords and extension cords to tables or baseboards.	( )
( )	6. Remove coffee table and other sharp-edged furniture from child's access and play areas.	( )

Bedrooms

To Do	Action	Done
( )	1. Install a night light for nighttime trips to the bathroom.	( )
( )	2. Move furniture and cribs away from windows.	( )
( )	3. Place safety locks on all windows and screens.	( )
( )	4. Make sure bars on cribs are no more than 2 1/2 inches apart.	( )
( )	5. Make sure mattress fits bed frame snugly.	( )
( )	6. Install bumper pads on inside of crib for young infants, the soft kind that bends or folds when stood on.	( )
( )	7. Remove mobiles over bed once child is capable of sitting or pulling to sit.	( )

Basement, Garage, Attic

To Do	Action	Done
( )	1. Throw away all old paints you're not using. Store paint thinners, paint, stains, etc. on a high shelf if you need to keep them.	( )
( )	2. Store all tools in a locked tool chest or shelved out of reach.	( )
( )	3. Lock all doors securely.	( )
( )	4. Keep garden tools, lawn mowers, snow blowers out of reach of young children.	( )
( )	5. Keep keys to electric machines safely out of reach.	( )
( )	6. Take doors off of old refrigerators and freezers.	( )
( )	7. Store pesticides and fertilizers on high shelves out of reach of children.	( )

General Safety Rules

1. Never leave a young child unattended in the bathroom.
2. Install smoke alarms and fire extinguishers.
3. Keep all matches and candles out of reach.
4. Post emergency numbers beside the telephone.
5. Never refer to medication as candy.
6. Avoid letting children play with small objects he/she can swallow.
7. Never leave a young child unattended in the basement, garage, or attic.
8. Keep ashtrays and cigarette butts out of children's reach. Nicotine is a deadly poison when eaten.

Safety Reminders By Age

1 month — **Crib Check**
Make sure there is no space between mattress and crib side for baby to get caught. Use bumper pads.

2 months — **Guard Against Falls**
Babies can roll over already. Never leave a child unattended on a dressing table or other high place.

3 months — **Car Seats**
Always use a properly installed car seat. If you also use the seat outside of the car, prevent falls by never putting it above floor level.

4 months — **Guard Against Choking**
Do not give young children small objects or pieces of hard food such as peanuts, popcorn, or hard candy. Learn the approved anti-choking maneuver for children from your pediatrician.

5 months — **Guard Against Scalds**
Babies like to grab and hit at things in your hands. Do not drink or carry hot liquids when near or holding a baby.

6 months — **Sitting Alone**
Baby may sit alone – but not in the bathtub. Never leave a child unattended in or near water.

7 months — **Safe Exploring**
Keep dangerous or breakable objects up and out of young crawler's exploring reach.

8 months — **Pulling Up**
Watch for falls. Check crib for areas where baby may catch his head or neck.

9 months — **Avoid Shocks**
Block electrical plugs with approved safety devices.

10 months — **Bigger Car Seat**
Switch to toddler car seat and use it every time child is in car.

11 months — **Burns**
In the kitchen, hot liquids, grease, and hot foods are a danger. So are irons, hot stoves, radiators, heating registers, and fireplaces.

12 months — **Stairway Safety**
Watch open doors and stairs. Use gates at top and bottom of steps.

13 months — **Walking and Exploring**
Beware of poisoning danger from houseplants, household chemicals, and medicines. Keep syrup of Ipecac, poison control phone number, and first aid chart and supplies handy.

14 months — **Climbing**
Children can now climb on chairs and tables – and find more danger. Keep medications and cleaning fluids out of reach. Use safety tops on all bottles and jars. Put locks on cabinets and drawers.

16 months — **Exploring Outdoors**
Define play areas and make them safe and interesting. Guard against scratches and bites from stray cats and dogs.

18 months — **Water Play**
Avoid hot water burns – keep water temperature between 120 degrees and 130 degrees F. Never leave a child alone in a tub or near any quantity of water – even a pail or a puddle – even if the child has had "swimming" lessons.

2 years — **Expanding Limits**
Start teaching good pedestrian habits and the limits of the child's "territory."

3 years **Riding a Tricycle**
Driveways and streets are dangerous. Allow riding only in fenced yards or playgrounds.

4 years **Venturing Further**
Teach good pedestrian habits—look both ways, stay out from between parked cars.

5 years **Bigger and Bigger**
You can now switch to seat belts for your child. Don't forget to "buckle up" yourself every time, too.

6 years **Riding a Bicycle**
Watch for falls. Teach good bicycle and street safety.

Teach good bicycle and street safety.

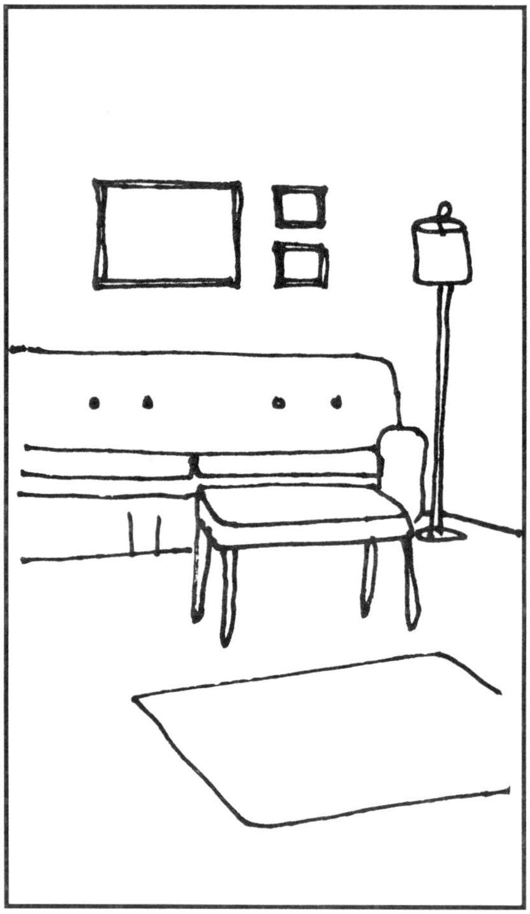

Provide a safe environment.

Make seat belts a habit.

Information from the American Academy of Pediatrics Committee on Accident and Poison Prevention, Growing Parent & Growing Child, October 1984, Vol. 12 No. 10, Dunn & Hargitt, Inc.

10

Verbal and Physical Redirection

Redirection is a technique designed especially for young preschool children that encourages them to perform desirable behaviors. Redirection is used by parents to:

- Prevent personal injury
- Promote desirable behavior
- Reduce punishing interactions
- Promote learning and exploration

Verbal Redirection

Verbal redirection is a means of managing your child's behavior by verbally expressing a command or request. It is a way to redirect the behavior of your child by talking to him. In the use of verbal redirection, a parent initially tells a child that the behavior that is occurring, or is about to occur, is not acceptable. A statement telling the child what is acceptable follows.

Appropriate Examples:

- "Chairs are for sitting. No standing, please."
- "No standing in the tubby. Sit, please."
- "Oh what a nice toy. Put it back on the shelf, please."

Inappropriate Examples:

- "No standing on the chair. You'll fall and break your neck."
- "Quit standing in the tub. What do you want, an accident?"
- "Yes, I see your toy. Now just don't leave it on the floor."

From the examples, you can see that the appropriate use of verbal redirection helps the child know what the parent expects and doesn't expect. The inappropriate use of verbal redirection actually doesn't redirect a child's behavior at all. Threats, statements of doom, and telling a child what not to do are not the correct ways to use verbal redirection.

Redirect unacceptable behavior.

Verbal redirection also includes directing the child's attention and behavior to other more appropriate activities and avoiding unnecessary confrontations.

Example:

Adam is about to run out of the bedroom when mom is trying to finish dressing him. She calls out "Adam, close the door for mom, please." Adam's attention is redirected from running away and he ends up complying and feeling like a helper.

"Thank you for helping, Adam."

This type of redirection works well with toddlers who haven't yet figured out that they are being redirected. It is not as effective after the age of three years.

Physical Redirection

Physical redirection is similar to verbal redirection with one added feature. As you are verbally redirecting a child, you are physically redirecting him as well. In the correct use of physical redirection, parents are using nurturing touch to redirect the child to perform more appropriate behavior. A hand gently placed on the child's back, or object taken from a child's grasp, or hand redirected from a dangerous object, are some ways parents use physical redirection.

Appropriate Examples:

- Physically redirecting a child away from an electric socket to a safe toy to play with.
- Escorting a child from the bathroom to the living room and engaging the child in play.
- Taking a dangerous object away from a child and substituting it with a safer one.

Use nurturing touch to redirect the child.

Inappropriate Examples:

- Physically jerking a child away from the electric socket.
- Spanking a child for entering the bathroom unassisted.
- Slapping a child's hand for touching a dangerous object.

Harsh and abusive touch is inappropriate.

In the appropriate use of physical redirection, a parent is using nurturing touch. In the inappropriate use of physical redirection, harsh and abusive touch is being used. The young preschool child is unable to make the connection between the harsh physical touch administered by the parent, and the danger to the object being touched. In the Nurturing Program, we believe the use of hitting, slapping, spanking, and other forms of harsh touch is abusive and has no positive value in helping a child learn appropriate behaviors.

Verbal and Physical Redirection Used Together

The ideal way to redirect a child's behavior is through the combined use of verbal and physical redirection. Used together, the child quickly learns that a particular behavior is unacceptable to his parents.

How to Use Verbal and Physical Redirection

1. In a firm voice, let the child know he is performing or about to perform an unacceptable behavior.

"Billy, NO!"

The firm voice indicates this is not a game; the NO indicates he is to stop the behavior immediately.

2. Approach the child, stoop down, make eye contact, and hold his hands.

3. Tell the child his behavior is unacceptable. Use words like, "icky", or "ouch", or "hot" if he is near something that could injure him like an electric socket, or hot oven. Use other words if the child has something in his hand, or is touching something you prefer him not touching. Words like "No", or "This is Mommy's; not for Billy", or "Sorry, this is not for little boys", convey the message. Used consistently, a child will begin to associate these words with certain behaviors.

"No Billy, ouch!"

4. Attempt to let the child re-establish the original setting. That is, if he has taken something, physically and verbally redirect him to return the object to where it belongs. If he has turned on an appliance, have him turn the appliance off. In this instance, you are encouraging the child to perform behaviors that are pleasing to you. Children like to please their parents.

5. The next step is the use of physical and verbal redirection. The goal is not to inhibit a child's natural curiosity, but to foster it through more appropriate activity. Engage the child in play. Some things young children like are:

   - keys and locks
   - putting anything smaller into something bigger
   - puzzles
   - coloring/scribbling on paper

   Make the activity you want the child to engage in so exciting that the child can't help but join you.

6. Praise the child for cooperating. Tell him he is a good listener. Praise for doing will reinforce future encounters. After all, you want your child to listen and cooperate.

Praise your child for cooperating.

7. If the child chooses to perform the inappropriate behavior again, repeat steps 1 through 6. A child is likely to repeat the behavior for two reasons: young children are too young to remember what was bad or good; and, some preschool children are likely to test you and the rule for consistency.

Children may test you for consistency.

8. Physical redirection is usually necessary and is more effective with younger children when their language is not as well-developed. Physical redirection should always be used in some form of verbal redirection. Also, physical redirection is used less as children get older, understand language better, and want to be independent.

Some Added Advice:

1. Never hit or spank a child as a means of physical redirection. Hitting is an abusive practice that sends a double message: I'm concerned about your safety, but I hit you and cause you pain and fear.

Choose redirection for behavior management.

2. We caution parents in the use of the word NO. Because toddlers like to explore, their whole world can become one big "No-No" if you let it. Save "No" for the big things. Also, when you do use the word "No", show an expression of disapproval. Slowly turning the head from side to side (physical indicator of No) and a cold, non-smiling face tells the child you are displeased. After a while, just shaking your head "No" gets the message across.

3. Baby proof your house. Get all the valued objects, stereos, tape decks, statues, cassette tapes, etc. above your child's grasp level. Life will be easier for you and your child.

4. If your child continues to want to perform the unacceptable behavior despite your efforts, it may be necessary to take the child to another room, or to spend more time with the child "to take his mind off whatever he wanted to touch."

Redirect to another room if behavior continues.

5. Finally, be consistent. A "No" is a "No" every time the unacceptable behavior appears. If you're inconsistent in the application of your redirection, expect your child to be the same. Spend the time and energy now in being consistent. You and your child will find living together an enjoyable experience.

Be consistent in redirecting your child.

11

Touch and Talk

Practice Statements

Talking to and touching your children teaches them many positive things about themselves. They learn that touching is nurturing and that adults are safe, fun, and to be trusted. Talking to your children promotes their intellectual growth and establishes a pattern of communication that will last a lifetime. Talking to and touching your children also lets them know it's OK to express their feelings, thoughts, opinions, and fears and that parents care what they have to say. Talk to and touch your children. The benefits will last a lifetime.

Touch and Talk

Practice Statements

This activity will help you become aware of touch as a means of healthy communication. It will also give you experience in giving and receiving praise. You will be doing this activity with a partner.

1. You are a nice person.
2. I like you.
3. It's nice to touch you.
4. I enjoy touching you.
5. I like being in this group with you.
6. I don't always feel this good about you.
7. Sometimes I get upset with you.
8. Sometimes I get angry at you.
9. Sometimes I don't like you.
10. I don't like what you are doing.
11. You hurt my feelings when you said that.
12. I felt sad when you did that.
13. I feel good when you are nice to me.
14. You usually are nice to me.
15. I like you a lot.
16. I feel love for you.
17. This exercise hasn't been easy, but I've enjoyed doing it with you.
18. I'm glad this turn is over.

"You are a nice person."

"I like you a lot."

12

Time-Out

Time-out is a form of behavior management used by parents to punish inappropriate behavior. A child is removed from the scene of the misdeed to a quiet area. There the child sits and does nothing until he or she is allowed to return.

What Time-Out is Not

Time-out is **not** isolating a child for long periods of time; it is **not** solitary confinement in some dark room; and it is **not** a threat of the loss of a parent's love or protection.

Inappropriate time-out.

When to Use Time-Out

Use time-out when the child has seriously violated one or more of the family rules. Some examples may be:

- deliberately breaking something
- throwing objects in the house
- ignoring a request to stop doing something
- abusive behaviors to others such as hitting, kicking, swearing, or pulling hair.

When Not to Use Time-Out

Do **not** use time-out for minor infractions of family rules, for behaviors you find partially annoying or unacceptable, or for normal accidents. Try ignoring the behavior or using other forms of behavior management instead of time-out. The selected use of time-out will increase its effectiveness as a management technique.

Before You Use Time-Out

1. **Make sure the child understands the concept of time-out.** Before using time-out as a form of punishment, make sure the child understands what time-out is and what is expected once he or she is in time-out. Using time-out before the child completely understands the concept is unfair and will only cause the child confusion.

Let the child know what time-out is all about.

2. **Establish rules that will warrant a time-out.** These should be family rules that all family members obey. If abusive behavior to others is not allowed in the house, this means both children and parents should not be abusive. If silliness at the dinner table is not acceptable, then everyone has to sit appropriately and eat their meal. It is important that parents follow the rules themselves, otherwise children will find the rules unjust. Modeling appropriate behavior is the best way to help a child manage his or her own behavior.

Establish rules that everyone will follow.

3. **Pick a time-out place.** The area should be without interesting things to do or look at. Sending a child to his or her bedroom would not be an appropriate time-out. A child's bedroom has too many things to do (read, color, play) or look at (television, magazines, pictures). On the other hand, a stairway (for children who can walk), hallway, behind a door, or a chair facing the wall are all appropriate possibilities for a time-out place. There's not much to do at these places except sit and wait. NEVER lock a child in a room, or use dark scary rooms, or rooms without sufficient air ventilation for time-out. Time-out is the removal of a child from a pleasant situation to a non-reinforcing situation. It is not a sentence to jail.

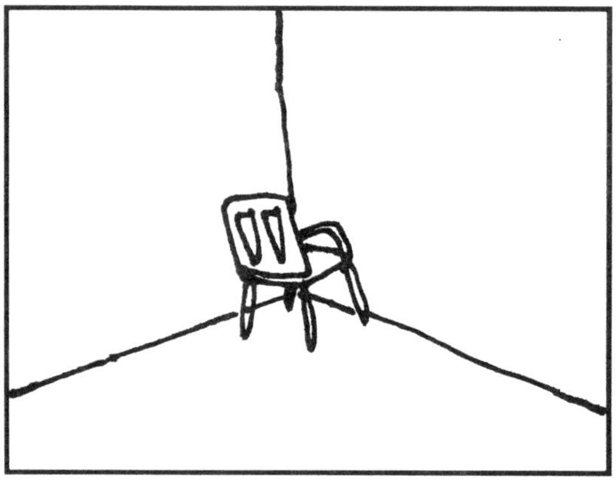

A time-out place should be uninteresting.

4. **Establish how long the time-out will last.** The precise amount of time depends on the age of the child and the seriousness of the offense. Generally, less serious behaviors get one to two minutes of time-out; more serious behaviors get three to seven minutes. Short duration time-outs (1-7 minutes) are more effective than longer time-outs (15-30 minutes).

How to Use Time-Out

1. **Give the child one warning that the behavior is inappropriate and that if it continues, he or she will have to take a time-out.** For example, you might say, "Tom, silliness is not acceptable at the dinner table. If you continue to act silly, you will have to leave the dinner table and take a two-minute time-out."

2. **If inappropriate behavior continues, tell the child to go to the time-out area.** If the child resists leaving, use minimum physical force to ensure the departure to time-out. Minimum physical force can be accomplished by gently, but firmly, taking a child by his or her arm, or under both arms near the shoulder, and encouraging the child to take the time-out. Never use abusive physical force to accomplish a time-out. The consequence of the inappropriate behavior is lost in the abusive force.

If behavior continues, time-out is administered.

3. **Ignore all comments, promises, or arguments by the child that she or he won't do the behavior anymore.** Any attention by the parent may reinforce the inappropriate behavior. Carry through the command to have the child take a time-out.

Carry through on the time-out.

4. **Tell the child how long the time-out will last. Be very specific.** "Tom, you have a two-minute time-out for acting silly at the dinner table after I gave you one warning. After two minutes of quietly sitting, you may return." It is not up to the child to determine when to return, or up to you to decide when you can stand him or her again. Time-out is a formal consequence to a formal family rule. If you have a kitchen timer, it is a good way to be accurate and to make the time-out objective. Remember to ignore any inquiries about when time-out is over.

Use a timer to keep the time-out accurate.

5. **Remind the child that time-out doesn't start until he or she is quiet.** If the child is loud, cries, or runs away from the time-out place, take the child back to the time-out place. Remind the child that the time-out period begins when he or she is sitting quietly.

6. **After the time-out is over, redirect the child to appropriate behaviors and praise the child for being quiet in time-out.** If the child had to be removed from the dinner table, he or she should be allowed to finish dinner. If the inappropriate behavior occurred during play time, spend a little time with the child modeling appropriate behavior for the play activity. If the inappropriate behavior occurs again, time-out must be readministered.

Some Points to Consider

- Time-out works best with pre-school and school age children. Time-out with teenagers is not a useful behavior management technique. Other management techniques such as choices and consequences and loss of privileges are more effective with adolescents.

Time-out is not as effective with adolescents.

- Time-out can be **voluntary** or **involuntary**. Voluntary time-out can be initiated by a child after an inappropriate behavior has taken place. Involuntary time-out is when the parent requests the child to leave the area after some misdeed.

A child can initiate his own time-out.

13

Ages and Stages

Development of Children

Developmental stages are periods of time children grow and learn new behaviors. At each stage, children are capable of doing only certain things because of their size, age, and maturity. The older they get, usually the more they can do.

What Kinds of Developmental Stages Are There?

There are four general kinds of developmental stages:

1. Physical Development

1. **Physical development** means that as children get older they usually get bigger. Usually when they get older and bigger, their gross motor and fine motor skills increase. Gross motor means activities like running, throwing, jumping, crawling, etc. Fine motor means activities like writing, holding a fork and knife, using a scissors, etc. Physical development is important for helping children not only increase their skills but also organize their behaviors.

2. Intellectual Development

2. **Intellectual development** means that children learn more the older they get. They learn to recognize shapes and color, recite the alphabet, figure out problems, and numerous other things. These intellectual abilities continue to increase as children continue to grow.

3. Language Development

3. **Language development** generally means that as children grow older, their communication skills increase. Their ability to use words, phrases, and sentences in writing and in conversation help them gain mastery of their environment by expressing their needs and understanding the needs of others. Language expands from a few simple sounds during the first year of life to the use of thousands of words in their teen years.

4. Social and Emotional Development

4. **Social and emotional development** go hand-in-hand. The way children are treated and the care they receive affect the way they mature and are capable of interacting with others. Children's emotional growth generally goes from an early stage of dependence and taking to a later stage of independence and giving.

Everyone Goes Through Stages of Growth

All children go through developmental stages as they grow and mature into adults. In fact, developmental stages continue right into old age. We all go through stages, some of us faster than others, and some of us more thoroughly than others.

Everyone goes through developmental stages.

A word of caution. No child is "average" in all areas of growth. Children are unique. Some are better at doing certain tasks than others. Development is influenced by the experiences and opportunities children have to learn, as well as the abilities they are born with.

What Developmental Stages Tell Us

At different times in our lives, from infancy to adulthood, we are capable of doing certain things like running, lifting heavy objects, talking, feeding ourselves, being able to care for someone else, etc. Developmental stages actually serve as rough guides for giving parents an idea when children may be capable of performing desired behaviors. They are not meant to serve as the final word on children's abilities. Not all children are capable of performing a behavior just because a stage indicates they should, but general knowledge of developmental stages gives parents a good idea what children may be capable of doing.

Why Learn About Developmental Stages?

We learn about developmental stages because we want to become the best parents we can. We also learn about developmental stages because it makes the life of being an infant and a young child easier and happier. Being an infant is not always that pleasant. There are very few things infants can do by themselves besides sleep, cry, wet and soil themselves, and burp. They even have to learn to turn over once they are lying on their backs. It's not simple. Life gets easier as infants get older because they can do more things independently.

But imagine if parents didn't know what infants or children were capable of doing at different times in their lives. Childhood would be a frustrating experience. We might be asking small infants to feed themselves, or young children to set the table, cook the meals, do the dishes. When such inappropriate expectations are placed on children, the children can't complete the task, and they begin to feel badly about themselves.

Parents need to have appropriate expectations.

Developmental Stages and Self-Concept

When we complete a task, no matter if it is a large or small task, we usually feel as if we accomplished something. People often notice our accomplishments and usually praise us for our efforts. The praise we receive helps build in us a positive feeling about ourselves or a positive self-concept. Trouble begins to occur when we constantly fail to accomplish something. No one recognizes our efforts and we don't receive any praise. In fact, we often receive just the opposite—criticism about how we can't do anything or how bad we are. When this happens often, we begin to believe we can't do anything and begin to feel badly about ourselves. A negative self-concept grows.

The importance of development and self-concept is extremely critical in the growth of children. A self-concept begins very early in life based on how capable we feel we are in pleasing our parents. After all, children want to please the very people they are dependent upon. When the expectations placed on children or infants are inappropriate, that is, children don't complete the task or do the activity because they are too young and don't have the skills, children see themselves as failures. Failures are children who can't seem to please mom and dad no matter how hard they try. When mom and dad are not pleased, they don't offer any praise. Without praise from mom and dad, it is nearly impossible for children to feel good about themselves and develop a positive self-concept. Without a positive self-concept, the chances of children trying new tasks or being successful are slim. This failure carries over to school where children will often see themselves as incapable and less bright than the other children.

"I can't do anything right!"

What is Important to Learn

Listed in the following pages is information about developmental stages that you should know. Having a good working knowledge of what your children can or can't do will help you in having appropriate developmental expectations of your children. In turn, you will encourage your children to meet success and reinforce positive feelings about themselves.

Knowing what to expect will lead to success.

Developmental Summaries

The following developmental summaries of children serve as a rough guide to normal child development. It should be noted that the lists serve only as a summary and are not a complete index of all the things children can do at any given stage. Children born with birth problems such as prematurity, low birth weight, or illness may not be able to do the things that other children can do who didn't have problems at birth. Most likely, such children will be behind and will need more time to catch up. Only with the support of their family will handicapped children, or children with special developmental needs, grow to the fullest of their capabilities.

14

Development Stage: Infancy

Chronological Age: Birth to One Year

The first year of an infant's life is both fascinating and startling. For years, psychologists have thought that babies were incompetent creatures who were unable to comprehend the world around them. Today we know that is untrue. At six to ten days, the newborn can recognize the mother by her smell. Some studies reveal that newborns can move their bodies in rhythm to the meaningful speech of adults. Babies at two weeks will look at their own mothers more frequently than they will look at strangers. It is apparent that very young infants can begin to make some sense of their new environment. As they grow older during their first year of life, their body language, intelligence, and social interactions also increase.

Physical Development

The major part of the infant's first year is devoted to survival. The infant is completely helpless at birth and is totally dependent upon the parents for help. Being fed, held, touched, looked at, and talked to have significant impact on the growth of the child. There is so much activity that the average baby sleeps from 16 to 20 hours each day. In fact, there is so much going on during the first year that it is impossible to notice everything. The first year is indeed an important one for the child's physical growth.

- Automatic reflexes such as hand-to-mouth. (0-2 months)

Hand-to-mouth reflex.

- Will use eyes to follow you. (2 months)
- Will lift head when on his stomach. (2 months)
- Sucks his fingers. (2 months)
- May be pulled slowly by hands to a sitting position. (2 months)
- May be starting to teethe. (4 months)
- Can sit up by himself for short time. (7 months)
- Can begin to crawl by pulling self forward with arms and dragging legs and stomach. (7 months)
- With help of furniture, can pull self up to stand. (7 months)
- Likes to pick things up and drop them only to pick them up again. (7 months)

Learning to play.

- Feeds himself pieces of food with hands. (7 months)
- Starts practicing walking but continues crawling. (10 months)
- Likes to eat meals using fingers, using one hand more than the other. (10 months)

Learning to feed self.

- Begins a tottering walk with legs wide apart. (12 months)
- Sits independently on hard surface. (12 months)

Intellectual Development

Physical and intellectual development are closely related to one another. The child learns about the world through exploration of objects, by moving around, and through interactions with the parents. Jean Piaget, a Swiss psychologist, helped us understand how children learn. He believed that intelligence involves adaptation to the world. Such adaptation means that the individual is capable of interacting effectively with the environment. The behavior of infants during the first year, and subsequent years, is to help them understand, adapt, and interact effectively with their world.

- The language of a newborn is crying. Crying occurs without tears for a special reason: to have his/her needs met. (0 - 2 months)

Infants cry to get their needs met.

- Reflex behaviors, like sucking, are practiced. (0 - 2 months)
- Begins to recognize familiar voices or faces. (2 months)
- Responds to strangers by crying or staring. (2 months)
- Likes repetition of simple acts like sucking, opening and closing hands, etc., for own sake of activity. (2 - 3 months)
- Baby still cries but also laughs out loud. (4 months)
- Can imitate sounds. Watches your mouth with interest when talking. (7 months)
- Child repeats an act to observe change in the environment. Baby kicks mobile to make it go. However, actions are not organized with a purpose; rather, the goal is discovered accidentally in the process of activity. (6 - 8 months)

An infant repeats an act to observe change.

- Follows moving objects with eyes. (0 - 12 months)
- Child uses responses to solve problems and to achieve some goal. For example, a child may move one object to get at another. (12 months)
- Responds to and imitates facial expressions of others. (5 - 12 months)

Language Development

Language develops very slowly during the first year of life. At birth, babies cannot say anything. By the end of their first year, the vocabulary increases to about three words. Even though language is not present during the first year, the experiences the baby has form a crucial basis for the development of language during years one through four.

Babies, however, do communicate their needs even without language. Crying is a way babies let their parents know they are either wet, hungry, tired, or frightened. Mothers and fathers soon learn the difference between a cry of fear and one of hunger. By the second month, babies begin cooing—a way of showing their pleasure. Babbling begins during the fourth or fifth months. Syllables are repeated over and over again. Parents who talk to their babies, praise and reinforce their efforts at communication, help facilitate the development of language.

- Responds to speech by looking at speaker. (0 - 12 months)

Responds to speech by looking at speaker.

- Makes crying and non-crying sounds. (0 - 12 months)
- Babbles by repeating some vowel and consonant sounds. (0 - 12 months)
- Attempts to imitate sounds. (0 - 12 months)
- Babies begin to "understand" many words or phrases such as "No, come, bring", etc. (12 months)

Social/Emotional Development

The stages of social and emotional growth are described by Erik Erickson. In the earliest stage, birth to one year, the child struggles with learning to trust or mistrust himself and others in his environment. The degree to which a child comes to trust the environment, other people and himself depends to a considerable extent upon the quality of the care the child receives. The child whose needs are met, whose discomforts and fears are quickly removed, who is held, loved, played with and talked to develops a belief that the world is a safe place, and that people are dependable and helpful. The child who receives inconsistent and inadequate care and who is rejected develops a basic mistrust of others, his environment, and self. For this child, the world is not a safe, fun place to be, and people are not to be depended upon to have needs met. Although the child is actively involved in developing trust or mistrust in the first year, the same issue arises again at each successive stage of development.

- Likes high-pitched voices and will usually quiet down when he/she hears them. (0 - 2 months)
- Smiles spontaneously. (0 - 2 months)
- Loves to be played with and likes to be picked up. (4 months)
- Responds differently to strangers (may cry) than to familiar persons. (4 - 6 months)
- Babies may give joyful kicks and gurgle and laugh to engage mother in play. (5 months)
- Knows that mother exists even though she may not be visually present. (5 months)
- May become attached to particular toy. Play time is important. (7 months)

Child may have a favorite toy.

- Child is beginning to learn to be independent. He or she may go a little away from you, but will quickly return. (10 months)
- Child will express anger (through crying) if some wish for mastering a task is frustrated. (8 - 10 months)
- Child loves an audience and will repeat any behavior that gets it. (12 months)
- Tantrums may occur. Based on needs and limited abilities, a child may desire to have or do something that cannot be achieved. (12 months)

15

Development Stage: Toddler

Chronological Age: One Year to Three Years

Life with toddlers is rarely dull. Their busyness, intensity, curiosity, independence, and increasing verbal skills make them both exciting and frustrating for parents. Parents are often pleased by some of the observations they verbalize, and sometimes outraged at their stubbornness.

This stage has often been called the "terrible twos" because of the child's increased needs to explore the surroundings and gain control over the environment. Both expressive language and physical mobility increase during this stage. The toddler is in a rush to discover his/her new style of living.

Physical Development

By the end of the first year, the average one year old is between 27 to 29 inches in height and weighs approximately 22 pounds. By the end of the third year, height has increased to around 36 inches and weight to 35 pounds. Although growth in the second and third years is slower than infancy, it still occurs at a rapid pace.

Toddlers are still growing at a rapid pace.

Large Muscle Development (Gross Motor)

- The child should be walking better. Feet are more parallel and can walk without holding arms up for balance. Child usually can walk backwards. (15 months)
- The toddler can pick up things from a standing position without falling. Now that hands are free, he loves to carry things, especially big things. (15 - 18 months)

Picking things up without falling is great fun.

- Child likes to push or pull toys, loves to throw things. (15 - 18 months)
- Seats self in child's chair; moves to music. (18 - 24 months)
- Runs, jumps, climbs, and stands on chair, walks upstairs, crawls downstairs backwards, kicks at ball, loves pounding, tugging, lugging, dumping. (18 - 24 months)
- Climbs small ladder. (around 36 months)
- Walks on tiptoe; stands on one foot with aid. (24 - 36 months)

Small Muscle Development (Fine Motor)

- Combines use of several objects: hitting one object with the other; dropping small things into large containers. (15 - 18 months)
- Begins to use spoon to eat; drinks from a cup that is held. (18 months)
- Turns several pages at a time; can make a straight stroke with pencil or crayon instead of just a scribble. (18 months)
- Can turn a doorknob, builds tower of many blocks. (18 months)

Toddlers can build towers with blocks.

- Turns single pages; drinks from a cup without help. (24 - 36 months)
- Removes shoes, pants, socks, sweater; unzips large zipper. (24 months)
- Snips with scissors; hold crayons with thumb and fingers, not fists; paints with wrist action, makes dots, lines, circular strokes. (24 - 36 months)
- Uses one hand consistently in most activities. (24 - 36 months)

Intellectual Development

The increased exploration and discovery of objects within the environment lead to activities that expand the child's understanding of the world. According to Piaget, at eighteen months, the toddler's interest is directed beyond his body. Toddlers begin to understand that each object has an independent existence and permanence. Such understanding leads to exploration of these objects and how they work. He learns that a chair remains the same whether seen from above, behind, or underneath.

From eighteen months to two years of age, children are limited to immediate experiencing of objects, people, and whatever or whoever else is present at the moment. A lot of time is spent staring at objects, people, or events as a means of exploration of the world. The beginning of language use and memory occurs around two years. By three, children are able to remember events, people, and activities they observed in the environment. Memory expands dramatically. It helps him to learn language. During two and three years of age, language develops rapidly, and imaginative and imitative play increases. Parents are often surprised at what children are able to remember and imitate later.

Memory develops dramatically at this stage.

- Toddlers are curious about textures—they like to stroke a cat or dog and rub their cheeks against the fur. (18 months)
- Toddlers are attracted to water and to toilets and enjoy playing in the bathroom. (18 - 24 months)

Toddlers like to play in bathrooms.

- Imitates actions and words of adults. (18 - 24 months)
- Recognizes difference between you and me. (18 - 24 months)
- Has limited attention span; accomplishes primary learning through exploration of environment. (12 - 24 months)
- Responds to simple directions "give me the block; get your shoes." (24 - 36 months)
- Recognizes self in mirror; can talk briefly about what he is doing. (24 - 36 months)

"Hey, that's me!"

- Has limited sense of time: vaguely knows idea of past and future and knows such terms as "yesterday" and "tonight," although they may be used incorrectly.

Language Development

Babies begin to produce a few basic words at about a year of life. By 24 months, most children are speaking phrases and have a wide range of words. A two-year old has a vocabulary of perhaps 50 words, which increases to about 900 words by the time the child is three.

Many factors contribute to the development of language in a child. A strong, emotional relationship with mother, enhanced by the amount and quality of time spent together, and the amount of talking, asking questions, and responding to what the child says increases the child's verbal activities.

Strong relationships enhance verbal activities.

- Says first meaningful words. (12 - 24 months)
- Uses single word plus a gesture to ask for objects. (12 - 24 months)
- Refers to self by name; uses "my" or "mine" to indicate possession. (12 - 24 months)
- Toddler likes to talk to self; replaces baby language with sentences; likes to repeat words. (24 months)
- Joins words together in two word phrases, e.g. "see doggy." (24 months)
- Asks what and where questions. (24 - 36 months)

Social/Emotional Development

Autonomy vs. Doubt

Parents of toddlers have an overwhelming job. The child continues to be needy and dependent, but at the same time is growing and developing into an independent person both physically and emotionally. According to Erickson, the second and third years of a child's life focus on the emergence of **autonomy**. This autonomy is built upon the child's new motor and mental abilities. The child takes pride in his new accomplishments and wants to do everything himself. Whether it is pulling the wrapper off a piece of candy, wanting to dress himself, or flushing the toilet, the child wants to demonstrate his competence at completing the task.

Toddlers want to be independent.

The importance of the stage reflects upon the willingness of parents to allow the child to express his autonomy. If parents are impatient and do for the child what he is capable of doing, they create a sense of shame and doubt. Overprotecting, abusive treatment, criticizing, and inappropriate expectations foster feelings of "I'm not capable" or "I'm not worthy." Such doubt or shame will handicap a child's attempts to achieve autonomy in adolescence and adulthood.

"I can do it myself!"

Parents need to help a child explore and grow during this stage. To accomplish this task, parents can:

1. Provide a safe environment for the child to explore. "Baby proof" the house. Remove breakables and eliminate hazards.

"Baby proof" your house for a safe environment.

2. Provide a creative environment for the child to explore. Use creative toys and games to facilitate learning.

3. Be involved in the child's exploration. Talk to the child to reinforce natural curiosity and exploration of the environment.

Problems

Special social/emotional problems arise during this time that will be briefly discussed.

Separation From Parents

Children quite frequently get upset at separation from the parents, particularly from mother. The emotional tie that is developed between mother and child results in the child wanting to be with the parent. Crying at separation is normal. Throwing temper tantrums at separation is a sign of possible problems.

Research has shown that children who are positively attached to their mother develop a sense of trust and feelings of security. Securely attached toddlers are outgoing preschoolers who are well-liked, attack new problems vigorously and positively, and can accept help from others. They are sympathetic to others, self-directed and goal-oriented, and exhibit high self-esteem and self confidence.

Toddlers who are not positively, emotionally attached to the parents, particularly to the mother, exhibit problem behaviors. Such children are anxious, throw more tantrums when presented with problems, are more negative in response to mother, ignore and oppose her in many ways. Children who feel less securely attached to mom fear separation. The fear can turn into panic during actual separation. To minimize the fear, a strong attachment needs to be established between mother and child. Feelings of security need to be developed, and assurances that mother will not abandon the child need to be expressed.

Strong attachment will reduce fear and panic.

Assertiveness

As the toddler becomes more aware of self, more independent, more definite in what he can and cannot do, the child will become more assertive in interactions with parents and peers. "No" becomes a common word. "I want," "I need," and "More" are other phrases and words frequently expressed in the toddler years. Children also like to command parents, sometimes adopting dictatorial tones of "Do this" or "Do that!"

Toddlers like to dictate to others and parents.

Assertion turns to frustration and anger when the toddler cannot accomplish what he or she set out to do. When parents exert limits (discipline) designed to manage the child's behavior, the child may express his anger physically—yelling, crying, temper tantrums, holding breath, or throwing objects. The physical activities release the tension that the child cannot express in words. Consistent application of ignoring undesirable behavior, praising desirable behavior, and punishing unacceptable behavior through time-out, loss of privilege, etc. will help the toddler negotiate this stage of development. As children become more capable and competent at achieving their ends, the tantrums will decrease.

Toilet Training

Most experts agree that somewhere between 18 to 24 months, children are ready to learn toilet training. However, it is important for parents to know that, just like eating, toileting is an area that parents cannot control, and the first area children learn that they can control. Therefore, in an extreme struggle of wills in toilet training, the child will win. An approach that helps the child lessen his need to control this area is generally more successful. Several hints are offered:

1. Three guidelines exist for determining a child's readiness for toilet training:

   - Bladder control—the ability to stay dry for several hours

   - Physical readiness—the ability to get to the toilet and pull pants down

   - Instruction readiness—the ability to understand instructions and communicate needs

Check guidelines to determine readiness.

2. Don't make a big deal out of toilet training. Do not talk about it much, or give much praise. The child can use the achievement to frustrate parents if he gets angry.

3. Establish a toilet routine. There are many books available on how to establish such a routine.

Establish a good toilet routine.

4. Use a potty chair. It is less frightening than a toilet.

A potty chair feels safer to a toddler.

5. Have the child observe the parent or sibling in the bathroom as a model.

16

Development Stage: Preschool

Chronological Age: Three Years to Six Years

The preschool period in a child's life is an exciting time. During this time, the child reaches out to the world beyond his/her home. For them, the world is an exciting place with many things to do, to touch, to experience, and to eat. Although the preschool child cannot read, write, or compute logical processes, the quest for knowledge overrides any developmental limitations. The preschool years set the stage for experiences, friends, and accomplishments obtained outside the home.

Physical Development

In comparison to earlier stages of development, the physical growth of the preschool child has slowed down considerably. Nevertheless, preschoolers usually gain 2 1/2 to 3 inches in height each year, and three to five pounds in weight. By the age of five years, preschoolers are generally 42" tall and 40 to 45 pounds in weight. The physical growth of the brain achieves about 90% of its adult size around the age of five years.

The growth of the brain facilitates control of voluntary movements. Old skills are refined and elaborated, and are put to new use. The basic motor abilities are present.

Large Muscle Development (Gross Motor)

- Takes longer steps when running or walking. (5 years)
- Catches large ball. (4 - 5 years)
- Skips on one foot. (4 -5 years)
- Hops on one foot. (4 -5 years)
- Many can broad jump 28 to 35 inches. (5 -6 years)

Preschoolers can catch a ball and hop.

Small Muscle Development (Fine Motor)

- Children can draw, use scissors, and begin to color. (4 -6 years)

Preschoolers begin to draw, color, and cut.

- Can get close to drawing a person. (5 years)
- Can begin to read, write. (5 - 6 years)
- Copies shapes—can draw square and triangle, probably not a diamond. (5 - 6 years)
- Can paint with broad strokes. (5 -6 years)

Intellectual Development

Preschoolers are intellectually curious and actively seek to learn as much about their environment as they possibly can. According to Piaget, the child is in a stage where he/she learns to represent objects, persons, and perceptions with symbols. Thus, the beginnings of functional language. The child is no longer tied to what is physically present.

Functional language begins during this stage.

Questions begin during the preschool years, first about the names of objects and activities, then about the purpose of routines. Increased questions, dreams, nightmares, and fantasy in play are all indications of advances in intellect.

During the preschool period, children believe everything exists for a purpose, even themselves. As such, the child's questions usually reflect such interest: "Mommy, why is there rain? Where do babies come from? Where was I before I was born? Do I have to die?" David Elkind, a noted child psychologist, suggests that parents answer such questions in terms of purpose or function. "It rains to make the trees and flowers grow; babies come from mommies; before you were born, you were just a thought with your mommy and daddy; we all get old and eventually have to die." When the child receives a response that suggests a function or purpose, he is usually satisfied.

"Daddy, where did I come from?"

Preschool children have limited concepts of things and only pay attention to a small number of characteristics. For example, if they see water poured from a short fat glass to a tall thin one, the children will say there is more water in the tall one even though no water has been added. Preschoolers cannot easily understand relational terms such as "longer" or "smaller" unless the objects compared are very different.

Language Development

Preschool children are active conversationalists. As they develop intellectually, their language usage increases.

- Vocabulary of about 900 words at three years, 2,000 words at five to six years.
- By the age of five years, children use complete sentences strung together with conjunctions.
- Although they speak clearly, children will have problems with pronunciation and stuttering. These problems are usually temporary and a normal part of development.
- Experiments with sounds, often making up rhyming words. (3 - 6 years)

Preschoolers experiment with rhyming words.

- Uses "because, how, why" in his efforts to interpret cause and effect. (4 -6 years)
- Conversations tend to be one-sided. (4 - 6 years)
- Children love to giggle with "toilet talk," i.e. words such as "poo poo, pee pee," etc. It's not until years later that children learn to adapt conversation to suit the company.

Preschoolers giggle over toilet talk.

Social/Emotional Development

Preschoolers are highly social beings. They are ready to reach out and interact with other children in a more responsive fashion. A sense of self as a person; an "I" who thinks, feels, and acts is ready to interact in a more assertive way with his/her environment.

Preschoolers have a sense of self as a person.

Initiative vs. Guilt

The social dimension that appears during this stage is **initiative**, at one pole, and **guilt** at the other. According to Erickson, children initiate activities due mainly to their gaining mastery of the abilities. This holds true for motor, language, and play activities.

Whether the child will leave this stage with a sense of initiative or sense of guilt depends to a considerable extent on how parents respond to self-initiated activities. Children who are given freedom to initiate motor, language, and play activities have their sense of initiative reinforced. On the other hand, if the child is made to feel his/her motor activities are bad, questions are a nuisance, and play is silly or stupid, guilt over self-initiated activities will develop that could persist through later life stages.

Play/Imaginary Friends

By age five, children can play cooperatively in a small group. When children aren't available to play with, they invent imaginary companions to fill the void. Imaginary friends are fairly common beginning around age three. Children who have imaginary companions are often bright, creative, verbal, more cooperative, and more aggressive than children who do not. The existence of imaginary friends suggests that children generate the kinds of experiences they need for their own development that the environment cannot provide.

Imaginary friends are fairly common.

Sex Roles and Identity

Most preschoolers play with both boys and girls, but by age six prefer friends of their own sex. Girls imitate their mothers; boys try hard to act like men.

This stage is described as the time the Oedipal complex emerges. According to Freud, the child desires to be romantically involved with the parent of the opposite sex – to marry that parent and to have children. Preschool girls can be coy and charming to dad, while preschool boys can be protective and seductive with mom. During this period, preschoolers often feel competitive with the same sex parent, sometimes wishing the parent dead. Parents should remain supportive and understanding of the child. Eventually, the sexual identities change where sons and daughters often wish to be just like dad and mom.

Nighttime Wetting

Children usually have learned to be potty trained around three years of age. However, accidents can happen and do, usually at night.

Nighttime wetting is more common among boys than girls, largely due to the fact that the nervous system of boys matures more slowly. Ask the child how he thinks the problem could be solved. Some possible solutions are not drinking liquids after dinner, going to the bathroom just before bedtime, or not changing the sheets until morning. Again, the parents should remain supportive and give the child encouragement. Scolding or punishment will not solve the problem.

Be supportive, try to work on a solution.

Excessive Masturbation

Although masturbation is a normal behavior, excessive masturbation can be a concern. Excessive masturbation may be the result of an unhappy anxious child. Finding the sources of the unhappiness and anxiety, and correcting them, is a first step.

Often excessive masturbation in children results from not being a part of a social group. Providing many opportunities for activities with peers, helping the child achieve feelings of competence, and parental support often ends the problem.

Fears

Fears are a natural part of growing up. During the preschool years, children often fear animals, the dark, imaginary creatures, and natural events like storms, fires, thunder, and lightning. Parents who criticize a child for his fears, who are sarcastic, or even punish a child for having fears are not helping to reduce the fears. These tactics only tend to decrease the self-confidence and self-esteem of the child. A model of confident, nonfearful behavior, discussion of the fear, support, and understanding from the parents helps the child to understand the fear and eventually diminish the fear to a more manageable level.

Support and understanding help to reduce fears.

17

Skill Strips

Developmental Checklist

Knowing what to expect of your children as they continue to grow will help them develop a positive self-concept and positive self-esteem. Children love to please their parents as a way of saying thanks for your hard work and as a way of feeling successful. When children know they please their parents, they aren't afraid to try new things and to work hard at completing tasks.

Skill Strips

Match the skill with the correct age period. Circle the age you think children should begin to perform the behavior.

Behaviors	0-12 months A	12-24 months B	24-36 months C	36-48 months D	48-60 months E
Takes a few steps without support	A	B	C	D	E
Repeats same syllable 2-3 times	A	B	C	D	E
Builds tower of 3 blocks	A	B	C	D	E
Says 5 different words	A	B	C	D	E
Points to 3 body parts on self	A	B	C	D	E
Uses pincer grasp to pick up object	A	B	C	D	E
Imitates peek-a-boo	A	B	C	D	E
Pulls off socks	A	B	C	D	E
Holds and drinks from cup using 2 hands	A	B	C	D	E
Follows rules by imitating actions of other children	A	B	C	D	E
Snaps or hooks clothing	A	B	C	D	E
Pedals tricycle 5 feet	A	B	C	D	E
Attempts to help parent with tasks by doing part of a chore (e.g. hold dust pan)	A	B	C	D	E
Walks backwards	A	B	C	D	E
Will attend for 5 minutes while a story is read	A	B	C	D	E
Sucks liquid from glass using a straw	A	B	C	D	E
Imitates counting to 3	A	B	C	D	E
Puts on mittens	A	B	C	D	E
Holds up fingers to tell age	A	B	C	D	E
Uses word for bathroom need	A	B	C	D	E
Stands on one foot for 4-8 seconds	A	B	C	D	E

Skill Strips (Continued)

Match the skill with the correct age period. Circle the age you think children should begin to perform the behavior.

Behaviors	0-12 months A	12-24 months B	24-36 months C	36-48 months D	48-60 months E
Uses words: sister, brother, grandmother, grandfather	A	B	C	D	E
Stays dry all night	A	B	C	D	E
Takes turns with 8-9 other children	A	B	C	D	E
Draws a man (head, trunk, 4 limbs)	A	B	C	D	E
Engages in socially acceptable behavior in public	A	B	C	D	E

18

Handling Troublesome Feelings

Recognizing feelings in yourself and in your children is a very important skill for parents. Not all the feelings children and parents have are positive. Knowing how to handle troublesome feelings can make life easier for parents and children.

Handling Troublesome Feelings

1. The feeling I have the most trouble handling is ______________________________

2. When I feel ______________________________,

   my payoff is that I ______________________________

   or I don't have to ______________________________,

   or other people ______________________________

3. I am **most** apt to have trouble with my troublesome feelings when ______________________________

   ____

4. I am **least** apt to have trouble with my troublesome feelings when ______________________________

   ____

5. How I can handle my troublesome feelings:

   a.

   b.

   c.

19

Misery-Making Beliefs and Better Choices

Self-Defeating Beliefs and Their Alternatives

Misery-making beliefs only encourage parents to get down on themselves and to be their own enemy. Identify your misery-making beliefs and make better choices for a better life.

Misery-Making Beliefs and Better Choices
Self-Defeating Beliefs and Their Alternatives

Misery-Making Beliefs	Better Choices
1. It is an absolute necessity that I please all of my family, all of my friends, and all of my neighbors at all times.	I will do the best I can with my children and myself in my own way. If my family, friends, and neighbors do not like it, that is their business, not mine.
2. I must be a perfect parent and my kids must be perfect kids at all times or I am a wicked person who deserves to be severely punished.	I do not find my identity or my value in my children's behavior. I do not depend on their perfection for my own sense of worth.
3. When things go wrong, it is catastrophic, totally unacceptable, and I am a complete failure because everything is always all my fault.	It's a pain when things go wrong, but sometimes that happens. I'll try to do what I can to see things don't go wrong again the same way, but there will be other ways and there are some things which cannot be changed and so that must be accepted.
4. My child is already so bad there is nothing I can do to make things any better for this family.	My child's behavior has a purpose and I can influence it by understanding the purpose and making some changes in how I handle him/her and me.
5. I must solve every problem I have within the next 3 hours or I shall know for certain nothing will ever help and it is hopeless.	I will make one small change at a time and I will remember things take time to form and time to change.
6. I must feel warm and loving towards my child at all times or I am a bad parent, a totally worthless person and I'm out to kill myself.	I can feel however I want to feel. However, I have responsibility not to hurt my child whether or not I feel warm and loving towards him/her.
7. My house must be immaculate at all times. If it is not, that is the absolute proof of my total worthlessness.	Houses are for people and although I will try to keep my house fairly neat, I will value people more than the neatness of the house and this includes me.
8. If I am unhappy, tense, or any other negative feeling, it is obviously someone else's fault and I ought to be very angry at that person for making me unhappy, tense or anything else.	I can be unhappy or tense for no reason at all. I can accept responsibility for my own feelings and I don't have to blame someone else for how I feel. I can continue to function whatever my feelings are, knowing that they will change.
9. There is a perfect solution in every situation and if I don't find that absolutely perfect solution, it is catastrophic and I ought to kill myself for being such a stupid person.	I'll try a lot of solutions until I begin to find some which work better than others. Then I shall use those more often. I won't expect to find the "perfect" one ever.

20

Stress Management Techniques

Identifying and managing stress are two important qualities of a nurturing parent. Stress often leads parents to say and to do things that they later regret. It's when parents feel stressed out that they are most apt to resort to spanking and yelling at their children. Reducing stress helps everyone in the family get along better and live happier.

Life Stress Measure

Directions: Circle the number before each life event that has occurred in the past 12 months. Fill in the point value on the appropriate blank in the Points column. Add the points to obtain a total.

Life Event	Point Value	Points
1. Death of spouse	100	_____
2. Divorce	73	_____
3. Marital separation	65	_____
4. Jail term	63	_____
5. Death of close family member	63	_____
6. Personal injury or illness	53	_____
7. Marriage	50	_____
8. Fired at work	47	_____
9. Marital reconciliation	45	_____
10. Retirement	45	_____
11. Change in health of family member	44	_____
12. Pregnancy	40	_____
13. Sex difficulties	39	_____
14. Gain of new family member	39	_____
15. Business readjustment	39	_____
16. Change in financial state	38	_____
17. Death of a close friend	37	_____
18. Change to different line of work	36	_____
19. Change in number of arguments with spouse	35	_____
20. Mortgage over $50,000	31	_____
21. Foreclosure of mortgage or loan	30	_____
22. Change in responsibilities at work	29	_____
23. Son or daughter leaving home	29	_____
24. Trouble with in-laws	29	_____
25. Outstanding debts	28	_____
26. Spouse begins or stops work	26	_____
27. Begin or end school	26	_____
28. Change in living conditions	25	_____
29. Revision of personal habits	24	_____
30. Trouble with boss	23	_____
31. Change in work hours or conditions	20	_____
32. Change in residence	20	_____
33. Change in schools	20	_____
34. Change in recreation	19	_____
35. Change in church activities	19	_____
36. Change in social activities	18	_____
37. Mortgage in loan less than $50,000	17	_____
38. Change in sleeping habits	15	_____
39. Change in number of family get-togethers	15	_____
40. Change in eating habits	15	_____
41. Vacation	13	_____
42. Christmas	12	_____
43. Minor violations of the law	11	_____
	Total	_____

Adapted from "*The Social Readjustment Scale*" by Holmes, T.H. and Rahe, R.H., Journal of Psychosomatic Research, 1972, 142, 111-115.

Stress Management Techniques

Get organized: If you feel your life is out of control, you have too much to do and not enough time, you may wish to start here in developing your stress management skills. Briefly discuss each of the following:

- Valuing: What's really important? Are you spending too much time on non-essentials?
- Planning: Are you clear about what you want to accomplish and when?
- Time Management: Do you ever ask "Where did the day go?" Examine your habits. Do you procrastinate, deal with trivia first, jump from task to task?
- Pacing skills: Do you get behind and then work in frantic bursts? Do you schedule your time?

Change the scene: If you feel a need for more support, or if your physical surroundings cause tension, you may wish to try these stress management techniques:

- Contact skills: Humans need contact with others. Form supporting relationships by overcoming shyness, inviting someone in for coffee, introducing yourself to others.
- Creating a relaxing environment: Locate a place that is yours alone (at work or at home), decorate for comfort and atmosphere. Consider books, lights, photos, chairs, etc.

Improve communications skills: If you say "yes" to too many things, find yourself being misunderstood, or are feeling confused, take a look at the following communication skills:

- Listening skills: Do you really hear others? Listening alleviates stress by building a support network. Are you tuned in to others' feelings as well as their words?
- Assertiveness skills: Have you learned the art of saying "no"? Memorize "No thank you." Practice it without making excuses. Respect yourself.
- Fight: Swallowing anger eats up life energy and anger ferments inside. Is the issue worth fighting over? If it is, learn to fight fairly.
- Flight: The art of a graceful retreat can often buy time to regain your strength. Take care that this technique is not abused.

Adapt a new attitude: If you feel some of your stress may be due to self-imposed pressures or a negative outlook, these stress management skills may be helpful:

- Surrender skills: Accepting the present does not mean defeat. Let go of the past and learn to live within the limits set down.
- Imagination skills: Learn to laugh at life's incongruities. "When life gives you lemons, make lemonade." Do you always take the broadest perspective?
- Interpreting skills: How do you interpret an event? Do you change your crisis labels to challenge labels? Try to choose a more positive attitude and outlook.

Build your stamina: For those times when you need to meet stress head on, make sure your body is in prime physical shape.

- Get regular exercise: Exercise increases strength and stamina. Try exercising with a friend. It will provide support and make it more fun.
- Improve your diet: Stress and diet are closely linked. We all know what we should eat.
- Listen to your body: Minimize the wear and tear on your body by listening to its messages (stiff neck, headaches, etc.).
- Learn relaxation skills: There are many simple relaxation techniques. However, none are effective unless they are used.

Taken from Stress Management by Elaine Biech, Building Healthy Families, CESA 12, Portage, WI, 1984.

21

Establishing Nurturing Routines

A routine is a consistent way of doing things. Routines are usually established by parents to manage their own behavior, and the behavior of their children. Some family routines may be cleaning the home on Saturday mornings, doing laundry on Wednesday evenings, saying grace at the dinner table, etc.

A nurturing routine is a consistent way of doing things that promotes a child's self-concept and self-esteem. Nurturing routines are established by parents to reinforce the positive overall growth of their children. Nurturing routines tell kids that the way to do things in our family helps everyone feel good about themselves. And feeling good about yourself is very important for acting appropriately and doing good things.

Nurturing Routines Help Establish Consistency

Children feel secure when they know what to expect. The security they feel allows them to learn to trust people important to them, like their mother and father. From trusting parents comes the natural response of being able to trust others.

Nurturing routines help build trust.

Nurturing Routines Help Establish a Positive Self-Esteem and Positive Self-Concept

Positive feelings toward oneself and positive thoughts about oneself are two important personality traits which emerge from nurturing routines. Without positive feelings and thoughts about oneself, there is little chance that the child will treat others with respect and kindness. Since he feels and thinks badly about himself, it's likely that he will feel and think badly about others. Nurturing routines help develop in the child a positive regard for self which ultimately leads to positive regard for others.

"I like myself and you too!"

Nurturing Routines Help Establish Empathy

Doing something consistently, and doing it with concern for a child's self-concept and self-esteem, helps the child develop a sense of trust. Children learn that adults are people who care for them and help them get their needs met. This feeling of trust leads to feelings of caring for others as the child continues to mature. Empathy, the awareness of the needs of others, is a primary and necessary characteristic of nurturing parents and children.

Important Ingredients in Nurturing Routines

Nurturing routines consist of:

- Gentle, positive touch: hugs, kisses, tickles, massages

Gentle, positive touch is an important ingredient.

- Praise for being and doing: "Mommy really loves you" (being); "What a good listener you are" (doing).
- Happy, pleasant expressions and tone of voice: smiles; light cheerful voice.
- Caring, empathic caregivers: being aware of the needs of children.
- Fun: games, finger plays, songs, dance.
- Consistency: being predictable.

Types of Nurturing Routines

Nurturing routines can best be established in the following areas of parent-child interactions:

- Diapering and Dressing Time
- Feeding Time
- Bath Time
- Bedtime

Practice nurturing routines daily.

When is it Best to Begin Nurturing Routines?

Parents should begin to establish nurturing routines the moment they bring their baby home. Starting early is the best way to establish consistent, caring and loving parent-child interactions.

Start nurturing routines at birth.

The Nurturing Program helps parents learn to establish nurturing routines with their children, ages birth to five years. The next four sections provide information on four types of nurturing routines.

22

Nurturing Diapering and Dressing Routine

Diapering and dressing children are excellent times to use nurturing routines. During these times, parents can be encouraging enormous growth in the child's sense of independence and cooperation, as well as in positive nurturing touch. Let's take a closer look at how parents can establish a nurturing diapering and dressing routine.

Learning Independence While Dressing

Children like to do things for themselves as quickly as they can. You can see it very early when infants repeatedly try to stand and walk only to fall flat on their bottoms. You can also see it when they attempt to feed themselves by smearing food all over their faces with the hope that some of it will get in their mouths. Little successes in these and other tasks result in great joy because children are finally learning to do things for themselves. These accomplishments have greater value in that they help establish in children a sense of independence and cooperation. When independence and cooperation are learned, children learn to do more things for themselves and by themselves. But to help your children learn to be independent and cooperative, parents need to learn the major rule in dressing children:

Dressing and diapering children is a partnership between the parent and the child.

As a partnership, you and your children work together as a team in getting clothes on and off your child. The following steps are suggested to make dressing your child a pleasant experience.

1. **Let your children have input into what they will wear for the day.** You might do this by selecting two tops and two bottoms and having your child make the choice of which top and bottom to wear. In this way, your child is taking an active role in getting dressed. Also in a partnership, your child is taking an active role in getting dressed and undressed rather than the passive role most children experience. Too many parents dress or undress their child without the child's active assistance. The active partnership role builds independence and cooperation. Let's see how it works.

2. **Allow your children to do the things they can do by themselves without any help from you.** If they can put their socks on, fine, let them do it by themselves. If it's pulling up their pants, good, don't do it for them. Let them pull their own pants up.

"Mom, I'll do this myself."

3. **Assist your children in getting dressed but allow them to still have the lead.** In this step, you're only assisting your children in doing things they can't quite do alone yet—like, putting pants on, or putting a tee shirt on.

4. **Take the lead in assisting your children in getting dressed.** In the last step, you do the things your children are incapable of doing. It might by putting on and tying shoes, zipping zippers, buttoning buttons, etc. In step four, the child has yet to develop the skills to finish getting dressed that one day he will have. As your child develops more skills, the need for step four is less and less.

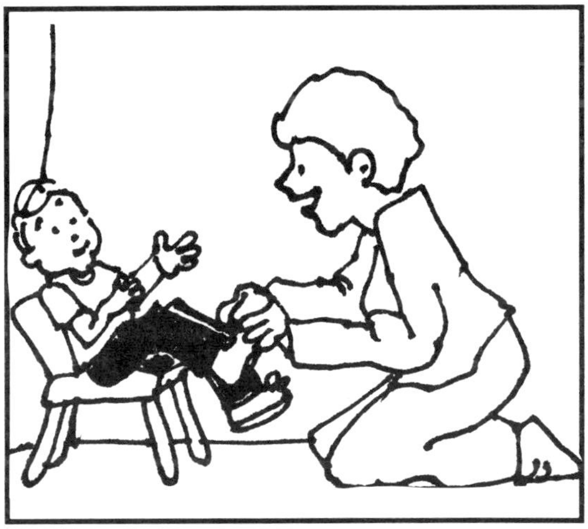

Take the lead in assisting your child.

Knowing When to Use the Steps

To assist you in knowing what steps to use and when to use them, here are some suggestions.

- Observe your child and make it a point to know what your child is capable of doing independently. The younger the child, the more quickly these skills will change on a daily and weekly basis.

- When you are pretty sure of the things your child can do by himself, break the things he can't do into smaller steps. The smaller steps will allow him to continue to gain further feelings of confidence. Let's take the activity of putting on a pair of pants. First, have him sit in a chair without you placing him there if he can do it by himself. Second, gather the pant legs and make doughnuts and lay them on the floor just in front of his feet. Third, tell him to step into the holes and ease the pants around his ankles. Fourth, have him take hold of one or both sides and "pull up." If he is very young, he probably doesn't have strength to pull the pants up all the way so you will have to help. Fifth, you do the snapping of the pants if it's something he can't do by himself.

Encourage your child to try new tasks.

Partnership Method Begins at Birth

Babies participate in the partnership method of getting dressed and many parents aren't even aware of it. When babies are getting their diapers changed, many children participate in the partnership method by laying still while mom or dad is putting a clean diaper on the child. Although this level of partnership may seem slight for the developmental level of the child, it is indeed very active.

Infants also participate in partnership.

Young infants also are active participants in getting themselves dressed by holding their arms and legs up, and by putting their arms through the sleeve openings. If you keep a sharp eye open, you'll notice all the things your young infant can do with a little assistance.

There you have it, the partnership method of helping your child get dressed. It takes a lot more time than getting your child dressed while they stand passively waiting for you to finish. However, the time you spend in establishing a nurturing dressing routine when your child is young will pay off later when your child is capable, cooperative, and independent.

Spend the time now for a positive pay off later.

23

Nurturing Feeding Time Routine

Eating is one of the most pleasurable times during infancy and young childhood. Babies love to eat. In fact, most babies double their birth weight in the first three to five months of life. That's a lot of eating! If they could talk, babies would probably tell us that nothing in this world is as good as sucking on a nipple and getting milk or juice. Watch them when they are sucking: they relax, begin to coo, close their eyes and fall asleep. Parents are probably pleased when babies eat because the child quiets down and is more pleasant to be with.

As children begin to grow older, something happens that changes all this pure pleasure into frustration, dissatisfaction, and stress for both the children and the parents. Children refuse to eat certain foods, are more attracted to "junk" foods, snack between meals, and begin to hate the very foods the parents feel are the best for them. What happens?

"Eat this, it's good for you!"

The Importance of Feeding Times

To begin to understand how feeding and eating begin to go sour, let's first discuss some common facts about children's eating habits.

- Despite some popular beliefs, babies know how many calories they need and what their stomachs can handle. If babies are not getting enough, they'll want more. If they get too much, they will stop sucking.

Babies know when they have had enough.

- Feeding is one of the earliest experiences babies have. As such, they begin to learn a lot about themselves and the world they live in. Good experiences in feeding lead to good feelings of self and the world. Bad experiences lead to bad feelings toward themselves and their world.

- Babies will normally lose weight immediately after birth, but gradually begin to gain back lost weight in two or three days. Such losses in weight are to be expected.

- Somewhere around a year old, babies begin to change their feelings about food. They become more choosy and less hungry. What might look good to eat today won't look good tomorrow. Their choice of certain foods is the beginning of exerting autonomy and control of their lives.

"I don't like that anymore!"

- Teething often takes away children's appetites, especially when the first molars are beginning to come in.

- As children become more mobile (around one year), they may lose interest in eating because they often feel too busy exploring the environment and practicing new motor skills to sit still and eat.

Establishing a Nurturing Feeding Time Routine

The following steps are suggested to make feeding your child a more pleasant experience.

1. **Provide your child with a comfortable eating environment.** Putting young babies in infant seats and older children in highchairs securely stationed on a table (infant seats), or the floor (highchairs), helps provide the child with feelings of security. Padded cushions and straps to keep your child snug in the seat are essential.

2. **Allow your child the opportunity to reject food.** When you honor the request, you are reinforcing feelings of personal power. Remember, children know when they are not hungry, or when they don't like something just like you and I do. When you force your child to take "one more bite" of foods he doesn't like, you're actually setting up a conflict situation in which the child will end up the loser.

3. **Reinforce personal choice in eating.** Get in the habit of giving small portions. If the child wants more, he'll let you know. Making children sit at the table until they clean their plates does not build healthy attitudes toward eating.

4. **Try to get children to think of food as something they want, not something they need to reject.** One way to encourage positive attitudes toward food is to allow your child to eat larger than usual amounts of one wholesome food than others. Remember, the older the child gets, the more his attitudes and tastes are changing. Continue to offer servings of your child's less preferred food.

5. **Encourage your child to begin to feed himself around nine to ten months.** Practice with finger foods, bread crusts, and other foods. Children will want to pick up the food with their fingers. Let them. Expect a lot of accidental messes. If you're worried about the rug, put some plastic under the highchair.

Let your child feed himself.

6. **Encourage your child to use a spoon.** Give him reason to use it. At the beginning of the meal when he's the hungriest, let him try to get food on the spoon and into his mouth. Assist your child in feeding himself with a spoon. Praise his efforts; tell him how proud you are he is trying to feed himself.

7. **Don't worry about table manners.** Touching, smashing, squeezing, and smearing food is an early form of child's play. Don't punish your child or take his food away. Remember, building positive attitudes toward food and eating is nearly as important as the actual eating of the food.

Table manners aren't important at this age.

8. **Praise your child.** There are many behaviors you can praise; feeding himself, eating a wholesome meal, sitting patiently waiting for food, using a fork or spoon, wiping his face, etc. Remember, praise the behavior you want.

Nutritious Foods for Children

Vegetable and Fruit Group

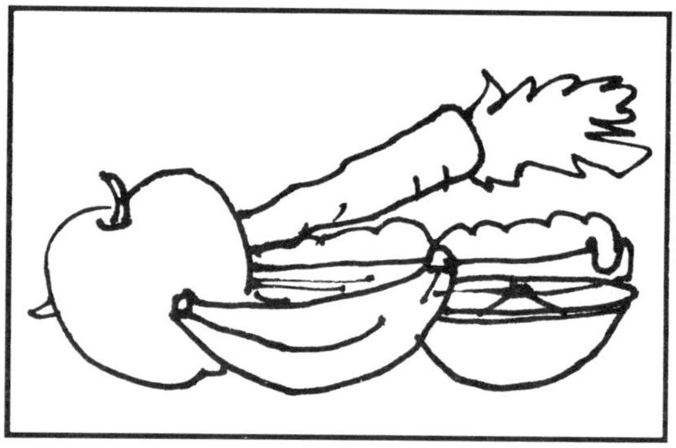

Quick and Easy!

Apples, peaches, pears, grapes, etc.

Raw vegetable sticks or pieces (radishes, celery, cauliflower, green onions, zucchini, green peppers, carrots, cucumbers – even parsnips!)

Dried apricots, raisins, prunes

Canned fruits or fruit juices kept chilled in the refrigerator

Ripe tomatoes – eat 'em right out of your hand!

Mini-kabobs of bite-sized fruit chunks, strung on a toothpick

Banana chunks dipped in orange juice. Shake in a bag with chopped peanuts. Spear with toothpicks

Celery stuffed with cottage cheese, cheese spread, or peanut butter

Juice cubes you make by freezing fruit juice in an ice cube tray. Chill other fruit drinks with them

Chilled cranberry juice mixed with club soda

Grapefruit half, sprinkled with brown sugar and broiled

Tomato half, sprinkled with breadcrumbs, parmesan or grated cheddar cheese and broiled

Creative salads of lettuce, raw spinach and other fresh vegetables, fruits, meats, eggs, or seafood

Bread and Cereal Group

Quick and Easy!

Raisin bread, toasted and spread with peanut butter

Sandwiches using a variety of breads – raisin, cracked wheat, pumpernickel, rye, black

Date-nut roll or brown bread spread with cream cheese

English muffins, served open-faced for sandwiches such as hot roast beef or turkey, chicken salad, sloppy joes

Individual pizzas. Top english muffin halves with cheese slices, tomato sauce and oregano, and broil

Waffles topped with whipped topping and strawberries

Wheat or rye crackers topped with herb-seasoned cottage cheese, cheese or meat spread, or peanut butter

Graham crackers and milk

Ready-to-eat cereals right out of the box!

Ice cream or pudding, sprinkled with crisp cereals or wheat germ

Meat, Poultry, Fish, and Beans Group

Quick and Easy!

Nuts, sesame seeds, or toasted sunflower seeds

Sandwich spread of peanut butter combined with raisins or chopped dates

Peanut butter and honey spread on an English muffin, sprinkled with chopped walnuts, and heated under broiler

Grilled open-faced peanut butter and mashed banana sandwich

Tomatoes stuffed with egg salad

Melon wedges topped with thinly sliced ham

Sandwich of cheese, meat, tomato, onion, and lettuce

Antipasto of tuna, shrimp, anchovies, hardcooked eggs and assorted vegetables

Leftover poultry or meat – as is, or chopped into a sandwich spread

Bite-sized cubes of broiled beef, served on a toothpick

Milk and Cheese Group

Quick and Easy!

Milk shakes with mashed fresh berries or bananas

Parfait of cottage cheese, yogurt, or ice milk combined with fruit, sprinkled with chopped nuts, wheat germ, or crisp cereal

Dips for vegetable sticks. For fewer calories, substitute cottage cheese or plain yogurt for sour cream and mayonnaise in preparing dips

Fruit-flavored yogurt

Cheese cubes, au naturel, or speared with pretzel sticks, or alternated with mandarin orange sections on a toothpick

Custard or pudding

Ice milk sundae, topped with fresh canned, or frozen fruits

Taken From: Food, Home and Garden Bulletin Number 228; prepared by Science and Education Adm., U.S. Department of Agriculture

Tips For Cooking With Children

1. Do your food prejudices show? **You** are the model; don't let your likes and dislikes influence the selection of food experiences.

2. Objective: To encourage the consumption of a variety of wholesome foods through positive experiences with foods.

3. Stress food in its natural state. Allow children to see, smell, feel, and taste the food at different stages of preparation. Compare colors and textures, shapes and sizes.

4. Choose simple cooking experiences first. As children master basic manipulative skill, gradually add more learning steps.

5. Develop "picture recipes" including utensils and illustrated measurement of ingredients.

6. Review the picture recipe and all directions before beginning a food activity.

7. Have all utensils ready ahead of time.

8. Sanitation: Does everyone have clean hands? Wash hands and work surface before starting. Explain what to do if child has to sneeze or cough.

9. Safety: Teach for awareness of sharp objects and hot surfaces. Children use knives and graters only under close supervision.

10. Supervision: Recommendation of one adult to every five to six children.

11. Planning: Coordinate cooking (food activities) with the class day. Build a food experience into multi-learning experiences—math, art, science, language, social science, safety, courtesy, **and nutrition.**

Choose simple recipes.

Prepare in advance.

Keep groups small.

Nutrition Education and Training Program
Food and Nutrition Services Section
Wisconsin Department of Public Instruction

24

Nurturing Bath Time Routine

For many young children, getting into a bathtub of warm water is not one of their favorite things to do. But, almost all children love to walk in standing puddles, splash water on others, and run through open sprinklers. So why is bath time a time of frustration, tears, and stress for the children and their parents? Let's examine why.

Why is Bath Time a Bad Time?

There are several reasons why your son or daughter may experience bath time as a bad time.

- **Most bath times come at the end of the day.** Not only may young children be overtired, but parents may be feeling the stress of their day and communicate this stress by being a bit more demanding that their children cooperate. Children easily pick up on the parent's anxiety and become anxious themselves.

Is this bath time at your house?

- **Because taking a bath comes at the end of the day, bath time is usually followed by bedtime.** Children soon learn that taking a bath means soon they will have to go to bed. If a child wishes to stay up longer, the obvious is to resist taking a bath.

- **Many parents treat bath time as a chore rather than a time for fun, relaxation, and enjoyment.** An attitude of "having to take a bath" is established rather than an attitude of "wanting to take a bath."

- **Bath time for children in some families is often an "on again-off again" occurrence.** Sometimes children have to take baths, sometimes they don't. Although parents may have good rationale for excluding a child's bath, children, especially young children, don't understand why on some days they have to take a bath and on other days they don't. What they experience is inconsistency. This leads to feelings of anxiety, which is then exhibited as resistance.

- **The experience of taking a bath may be a very unpleasant and frightening one for many children.** Soap in eyes, hot water burns, accidental falls, pouring water on a child's head to rinse hair shampoo, etc. are all things that can make bath time a bad time.

Bath time can be frightening to some children.

How to Make Bath Time a Fun Time

For children to want to take a bath more often than not, bath time has to be a fun time. The following suggestions are recommended for developing a positive, nurturing routine for giving children baths.

1. **Make bath time sound like a fun time.** Young children like to pretend; give the bathtub a name or refer to it as "tubby time" with a sound of happiness. Pretend the tubby can talk and call the child's name, "Chris, I'm waiting for you" and answer back, "We're coming tubby." It's quite a bit better than saying, "Chris, I want you to take your bath now!"

Bath time can be a happy, fun time.

2. **Let your child turn the water on and fill the tub.** Giving the child more responsibility in keeping himself clean is the ultimate goal. Start early by allowing him to put the bubble bath in, set the water temperature, and fill the tub to the desired depth.

3. **Encourage your child to play in the tub.** Bring in "tubby toys" for the child to play with; they don't have to be anything fancy. Use plastic cups, bowls, empty plastic dish detergent containers or plastic syrup containers with the plastic pour spouts, etc. Anything that floats, squirts water, holds or pours water will work.

Provide some toys for your children to play with.

4. **Encourage your child to get to know his/her body.** Tubby time is a great time for body exploration and recognition of body parts. Give your child's body parts names and use the names when washing your child: "Look, I see Adam's hands. Oh, boy! Adam's hands need a washing!"

5. **Take a bath with your child(ren).** Children think it's great fun taking a bath with their mom or dad. Singing, playing with toys, and washing all help the child feel more comfortable when mom or dad are also in the tub.

Hop in the tub with your children.

6. **Make the experience of tubby time enjoyable.** Several things you can do to help make the experience of taking a bath more enjoyable:

   - Use mild soaps and shampoos to avoid eye sting.
   - Place a mat on the bottom of the tub to prevent accidental slipping.
   - Protect against accidents by placing foam rubber guards over the water spout.
   - Get each of your children their own towel to dry themselves and their own robe to wear after taking a bath.

7. **Make tubby time a daily routine.** If children know that every day they will have a tubby time, soon they will come to accept it as a daily routine. Consistency will help lessen the uncertainty and reduce the anxiety of not knowing.

Words of Caution

- Never, ever, leave a very young child alone in the bathtub. Accidental drowning and other injuries can occur in a matter of seconds and minutes.
- Keep all electrical appliances unplugged and away from the grasp of children. Water and electricity are deadly together. For the sake of your family's welfare, keep all electrical appliances safely stored in a locked cabinet or closet.

Remove all electrical appliances.

25

Nurturing Bedtime Routine

At some point in almost every child's life, getting ready for bed and going to sleep are two of the least favorite things children are going to want to do. Much to the heartache of many parents, trying to get children to take naps and to get plenty of sleep often results in a lot of stress and frustration for both the children and the parents. Not surprisingly, in some families, bedtime becomes a battle time, where parents and children both end up losing.

Many experts believe that bedtime is one of the most important times for children to learn positive feelings about themselves and others in their world, in particular mom and dad. Unfortunately, because a lot of arguing and tension exists between parents and children during bedtime, what is learned and established is not positive at all. Establishing a nurturing routine at bedtime, one in which parents and children feel good about themselves and toward each other, is very important. Before we discuss how to establish a nurturing bedtime routine, let's examine why bedtime problems occur.

Bedtime Problems

Probably the single biggest contributing factor for young children to dislike going to bed is the anxiety they feel in being separated from their mothers. Remember, moms are very important to children for their survival. When they are not in view of the infant, feelings of fear set in. The term that is used to describe this fear is "separation anxiety." Separation anxiety results when children fear being left alone or unattended. Excessive crying and temper tantrums are two common behaviors associated with separation anxiety. Letting children know that you haven't abandoned them at nighttime is very important in helping the child build feelings of trust and security. Reassuring the child with kind words and a gentle touch helps reduce anxiety. As children get older, their fears of separation generally lessen and nighttime becomes a more peaceful time.

Separation anxiety needs kind reassurance.

Infants face another type of nighttime problem, one a little bit easier to solve. The problem is hunger. Infants get hungry during the night and need to be fed. Usually when fed, the baby will fall back asleep only to awaken when he's hungry again.

Many children three years and older have difficulty going to sleep at night because of nighttime fears. Wetting for children who are potty trained may be a sign of nighttime fears. Ghosts, boogeymen, monsters, and demons are all very real for some children who feel vulnerable at night. Nightmares may result, which only tend to reinforce a child's fear of the dark. In this sense, children don't want to go to sleep because they are afraid and insecure. Talking about their fears and getting older generally help children overcome them.

Another reason why some children may be reluctant to go to bed has more to do with what else is going on in the house. If nighttime is a time when the entire family plays games together, or favorite guests come over, or favorite television programs are on, children may not want to go to bed because they would rather be up having fun. In this instance, children feel they are being excluded from the fun. To avoid this situation, make sure all family play time occurs before bedtime for the youngest child.

Include all children in family activities before bedtime.

Lastly, many children have a difficult time sleeping in their own room at night because of the time spent there as a punishment during the day. Being "sent to your room", where some children have to stay for hours, does not encourage children to associate their room with happy, pleasant feelings. Rather, their rooms may be thought of as prisons where children are locked up for being bad. Avoid using the child's bedroom as a place to carry out a punishment. If you're using time-out as punishment, use the living room or kitchen, not the child's bedroom.

Building a Nurturing Bedtime Routine

To make bedtime a more pleasant experience, the following ten steps are suggested.

1. **The first step in establishing a nurturing bedtime routine is identifying a consistent time your child will be going to bed.** Inconsistent bedtime only creates confusion which ultimately leads to resentment. Identify a bed time and stick to it.

2. **Make a nice relaxing bath time part of the nighttime routine for going to bed.** A nurturing bath time routine will serve as a positive preview for what's to come in getting ready for bed.

3. **Dress your child in clothes (pajamas, sleepers, etc.) especially for bedtime.** Getting dressed in these clothes is an indication that it's getting close to bedtime. If you can get fun bedtime clothes with pictures of animals, or cars, or cartoon characters, etc. on them, getting dressed for bed will be even more fun.

Dress your child in bed clothes.

4. **Help the child get dressed for sleep in his bedroom, not in other rooms of the house.** Keep the association between bed, sleep, and bedtime clothes intact.

5. **Have your child brush his/her teeth every night as part of the bedtime routine.** What an excellent habit to develop at a young age. Model the way to brush teeth by brushing your own. Giving your child his/her own toothbrush to play with and use is strongly recommended as part of the bedtime routine.

Make it a habit of brushing teeth before bedtime.

6. **Spend time with your child reading stories.** Find a cozy rocking chair, have your child crawl up on your lap, get snuggled in, and read for awhile.

7. **Choose bedtime books that are happy and pleasing – books which add comfort not discomfort.** Save the scary stories for daytime reading when the child gets older. By the way, you might want to negotiate with your child how many stories you are going to read.

8. **When finished reading, tell your child it's time to lay down in the bed.** Putting your child in the bed **before** he is asleep is recommended. Some children who fall asleep in their parent's arms wake up during the night and wonder where mommy and daddy went. Putting him down before he is asleep serves to get the child used to falling asleep alone. Then nighttime awakenings aren't as scary.

9. **Tuck your child in, make sure you tell him at least one nice thing he did, or how much you love him as a person, give him a hug or kiss, and wish him good dreams.** If you can, sing a song or two, help him relax and get cozy.

Tuck your child in and say something nice.

10. **If your child should begin to cry during the night, go into his room, and find out what the problem is.** Remember, crying is a signal of distress. The child is asking for help. Find out what he needs. Maybe a bottle, a blanket, a little reassuring is all that is needed for him to fall back to sleep.

Bedtime Myths

There are a couple of myths about bedtime parenting practices that are passed on from one generation of parents to another without any real evidence of their harmful effects. These myths only tend to confuse parents and limit their ability to be nurturing parents. Let's examine these bedtime myths and present the facts.

Myth: Paying attention to a crying baby at night will only tend to reinforce the crying.

Fact: It will if the **only** time you pay attention to your child is when he is crying. Remember what you pay attention to is what you get more of. If you pay a lot of attention to your child when he is not crying, his need to cry to get attention is lessened. Contrary to popular belief, a child whose needs are met and who receives a lot of attention will stand a better chance of feeling secure and trusting.

Pay attention to the behaviors you want to see.

Myth: Never let your child sleep in your bed; you'll never be able to get him out.

Fact: Children like to feel close to their mom and dad. Feeling close is necessary in building trust and security. Occasionally crawling in bed with mom and dad because of illness, feeling scared, or just wanting to be close is okay. A daily habit of sleeping with mom and dad is not encouraged for several practical reasons: mom and dad need private time alone; staying up and reading or talking in bed might wake the child up; the size of the bed may not be conducive for three or more family members; and allowing a child to have his or her own private space is healthy for the child.

Sleeping with mom and dad is OK ocassionally.

Like all the other routines that are discussed in the Nurturing Program, establishing the bed time nurturing routine presented here takes more time and directed energy than a more inconsistent approach. The positive benefits of establishing nurturing routines, however, will be realized and enjoyed in happier, healthier family interactions.

26

Handling My Anger

Anger is a feeling of being irritated, teed-off, irked, annoyed, and furious. People get angry when they have been hurt. Everyone has angry feelings from time to time. Most of the anger people feel is not violent or difficult to control. Knowing how to handle your anger will model for your children an appropriate way to express their anger.

Handling My Anger

Write down your responses to the following statements.

1. One situation that occurs at home that often results in my getting angry is ______________________

   ____

   ____

2. When I am angry, I am apt to ____.

   When this occurs, I feel ____,

   and those around me feel ____.

3. One way I would like to handle my anger is ___________________________.

4. List three things you could do to handle your anger.

   a.

   b.

   c.

27

Rules for Fair Fighting

Arguing is a way two people let each other know they are displeased with the other. Although disagreeing with someone else is good, destroying the positive feelings of the other person and causing hurt are not healthy ways to interact with others. Following are some rules for fair fighting.

Rules for Fair Fighting

1. Decide upon a time limit before you begin and **STICK TO IT**. No more than 30 minutes, better if it is 15 or 20 minutes. If you don't finish in the amount of time allotted, schedule another time the next day.

2. Decide how many "zaps" you'll permit before you (or the other) walk out. A zap is a hurtful remark, an insult, a threat, a sarcastic dig, etc. If you feel you have been zapped, you have been. Any attempt to threaten, shame or blame is another zap. When you get to the number agreed upon ahead of time, walk out.

3. Choose one problem per session. Have a session every day for awhile if you need it, but stick to one problem per session.

4. Stay in the present. Don't bring up what happened 12 years or 12 days ago unless it very specifically relates to the present.

5. Stick to the point. Don't get carried away with other subjects. Focus on **one** problem per session, stay in the **present**, and stick to the **point.**

6. Own your own feelings. Avoid blaming your partner for your feelings; they are not anyone else's, they are yours.

7. Listen to the other person. You need both points of view to find an agreement for both of you.

8. Agree upon a solution which is good for **both** of you, not just one or the other.

28

Choices and Consequences

Choices and consequences is a technique used by parents to help children learn self-control, make wise decisions, help modify behavior, and develop independent thinking.

How Do Choices and Consequences Work?

Choices and consequences allow children, who are capable of knowing right from wrong, the ability to take responsibility for their own behavior. Simply speaking, children choose to act a certain way based on the expected consequences of their behavior. The consequences of their behavior strongly influence whether that behavior will recur or not.

Natural and Logical Consequences

There are two kinds of consequences to all behavior: natural consequences and logical consequences. These consequences can either be pleasant or unpleasant.

Natural consequences are not constructed or planned, but happen in the natural course of events. For example, a child who walks barefoot on hot pavement will have two hot feet. Playing with matches may result in burned fingers. A child who eats a lot of sweets and does not brush his teeth will probably wind up with a mouth full of cavities. No one has to plan them.

"Ouch! That's hot!"

Logical consequences, on the other hand, are planned or arranged consequences. Logical or planned consequences are established by parents as a way of helping children learn appropriate and desirable behaviors. There are three logical consequences that are widely used by parents: 1) Loss of privilege; 2) Time-out; and, 3) Restitution.

1. **Loss of privilege** may be used when children have broken family rules, refused to obey appropriate parental requests, or have misused objects such as toys, record players, or games. They may lose the privilege of playing with certain toys for one or two days; may lose the privilege of watching television for one night; or may lose the privilege of going out at night (being grounded).

2. **Time-out** is more effective as a consequence for pre-school and school age children than with infants or adolescents. Having children sit in a quiet area for five minutes is a powerful consequence for inappropriate behavior.

3. **Restitution** essentially means that children have to "make good" for an act they committed. For example, if a child breaks something on purpose, parents may require the child to "pay for" the broken object. Paying back may mean taking money out of his or her piggy bank, doing extra chores around the house, or replacing the broken object. Restitution is an effective consequence with junior and senior high adolescents.

The consequences mentioned previously are essentially punishments for inappropriate behaviors children chose to commit. Logical consequences, however, don't always have to be unpleasant. Rewards are also logical consequences for appropriate behavior. For example, when children complete their chores, they deserve to get their allowance. Extra treats, special times with mom or dad, or getting to stay up an extra half hour can also be positive logical consequences.

Allowances are logical consequences.

Choices

As adults, we make choices in our lives daily. So do our children. The kinds of choices that are made usually depend upon the outcomes or consequences we can expect. We learn from our choices. If we choose not to dress warmly in the wintertime, we will probably be cold. If we don't like being cold, we will make sure we don't leave the house the next time without dressing warmly. We make sure to dress warmly based on the discomfort (or natural consequence) we felt when we were cold. Children also make choices to act good or bad based on the consequences they can expect for their behavior.

Teaching Through Choices and Consequences

"Choice and consequence" is a very powerful teaching model for parents to use in helping their children learn desirable behaviors, particularly logical consequences, because parents have a lot of control over them. When a child learns that a particular behavior will result in either a reward or a punishment as a consequence to the behavior, the child makes a choice whether to perform the behavior or not. If the behavior has a logical consequence to it that is unpleasant, like staying out past curfew and being grounded the following night, the child is less likely to stay out past curfew—particularly if he wants to do something the following night. Hence, the child makes a choice based on the expected consequence to the behavior.

Rewards or punishments are consequences.

If You Promise, You Better Deliver

We have stated that children who know right from wrong make choices to act appropriately or not based on the expected consequences. To help children manage their own behavior, expected consequences have to appear after the behavior has occurred. If not, children become confused and don't know what to expect. For example, if you promise your son or daughter that they can have an ice cream cone after they clean their room, and they clean their room but don't receive an ice cream cone (the expected consequence is absent), the child is less likely to believe you the next time you promise anything.

Be sure to follow through on promises.

If your child breaks a house rule (no swearing) and the expected consequence is not there (time-out, loss of privilege, etc.) the rule has no meaning because it is not enforced. **The consequence of the behavior must occur each time the behavior does.**

Threats Are NOT Consequences

Parents will sometimes threaten children as a consequence for a particular behavior. Often threats cannot be carried out, and in most instances, shouldn't be carried out. For example, a mother is trying to vacuum the living room carpet. She notices her son has his blocks scattered around the floor. She could say, "Stephen, get in this room right now and clean up these blocks or you are going to eat every one!" Not a very good consequence. The response to the blocks on the floor is virtually ineffective. A better response might be, "Stephen, please pick up your blocks off the living room floor or you will lose the privilege of playing with them for the next two days." If the child likes to play with the blocks, and does so every day, losing the privilege of playing with them for two days would be disastrous.

Consequence Must be Related to Behavior

The consequence must be related to the behavior you wish to increase or decrease. Otherwise, the logical consequence can be perceived as unfair. The following are inappropriate and appropriate example of choices and consequences.

Inappropriate:

"Billy, you chose to break your toy by throwing it against the wall. As a consequence, you cannot eat dinner tonight."

Appropriate:

"Billy, you chose to break your toy by throwing it against the wall. Throwing things and breaking things on purpose are not allowed. As a consequence, you lose the privilege of playing with your toys for two days.

The consequence is related to the behavior.

Parents, Please Note

Choices and consequences only work when children are capable of knowing right from wrong, can perform the desirable behavior, and have the mental capacity to make knowledgeable choices. A four month old infant who soils himself after you told him he has to use the potty or else he can't have any juice is certainly not capable of either managing his bowel movement, or understanding choices and consequences as a means of managing behavior. This consequence would not be appropriate.

Abusive consequences are never acceptable no matter how severe the behavior. What the child learns after such actions is dislike for authority, a "get back" philosophy, and the idea that by hitting and yelling at kids, you can get them to do what you want. Such attitudes only lead to more abuse and more problems for the family. By using appropriate consequences consistently, children learn healthy ways to control their behavior.

Use appropriate consequences for behaviors.

29

Ignoring as Behavior Management

Ignoring is a form of behavior management used to reduce or eliminate behaviors of children parents find especially irritating. Ignoring is a way parents communicate their disapproval of certain behaviors by deliberately not paying attention in words or actions to undesirable behaviors whenever they occur. Not paying attention means absolutely no acknowledgement in any manner that the behavior is present.

What Ignoring is Not

Ignoring is not threatening, hitting, or criticizing children because of some undesirable behavior. To criticize a behavior, parents have to pay attention to it. To some children, any kind of attention, even negative attention is reinforcing. By paying attention to the undesirable behavior, parents are actually encouraging children to continue to perform the behavior.

Ignore undesirable behavior.

When to Ignore and When Not to Ignore

Parents may often wonder whether or not they should ignore certain behaviors. Certainly there are some behaviors that should be ignored and others that need the immediate attention of parents. Here are some helpful suggestions:

Degree of Potential Harm

Any behavior that increases the risk of physical harm to the child or other children cannot be ignored. Playing with matches or inserting objects into an electrical outlet are two examples of behaviors that cannot be ignored.

On the other hand, behaviors such as whining and temper tantrums should be ignored. It is highly unlikely that any of these behaviors will increase the risk of physical harm.

Damage To Property

Behaviors that can damage or destroy property should not be ignored. Writing with spray paint on an interior or exterior wall, stepping on plants, or breaking toys are behaviors that require immediate action. Other behaviors that have limited risk to the destruction of property can effectively be ignored.

Do not ignore destructive behavior.

Irritating Behaviors for Attention

Some behaviors that children perform are strictly for attention and most parents find these behaviors especially irritating. Nagging, quarreling, temper tantrums, whining, and interrupting are all irritating behaviors that children use to get mom or dad to pay attention to them. Paying attention to these behaviors will only tend to reinforce their continued use. Remember, temper tantrums are not likely to happen if there is no one to watch them.

There are some behaviors parents may find to be irritating that should not be ignored. Crying because a child is frightened or hurt is not a behavior that will disappear if ignored. There is a greater chance that the behavior will stop if the child is held and reassured. Crying during a temper tantrum, on the other hand, should always be ignored.

Before You Use Ignoring

1. Decide what behavior you want to see.

Decide what you want to see.

2. Be sure you can tolerate the behavior without eventually giving in or punishing the child.
3. Decide whether you can tolerate the behavior without having to remove the child from the area.
4. Ignore the behavior 100% of the time no matter how long it lasts.

Ignore the behavior no matter how long it takes.

How to Ignore

The following suggestions will help you learn the technique of ignoring.

1. **Ignoring means absolutely no attention.** Do not look at or talk to the child. Any attention, even threats and criticism, will reinforce the behavior. Focus your attention elsewhere. Dream your favorite day dream, plan your fantasy vacation, or relive a happy memory.
2. **The behavior may continue for one minute, 10 minutes, or 30 minutes. Ignore the entire time.** The behavior may turn for the worse before it gets better. If that happens, don't give in even though you may feel angry or embarrassed.
3. **When the behavior stops, praise the child immediately.** "I'm sure glad you stopped your temper tantrum. I don't like temper tantrums and it's much nicer to be with you when you aren't screaming." This is the good consequence. The child has now learned temper tantrums did not get your attention, but when he or she stopped, you gave your attention.
4. **If anyone else is reinforcing the inappropriate behavior, like a sympathetic grandparent, brother, or sister, you will have to convince them to ignore the behavior also.**
5. **When using ignoring as a technique in changing behavior, you do not ignore the child, you ignore the irritating behavior.** The child soon gets the message that even though you love him or her, you do not like the undesirable behavior.

Remember—praise the behavior you like, ignore the behavior you don't like.

30

I Statements and You Messages

I statements are expressions about me. These expressions can focus on how I feel, on what I need, or about what I think. For example, I statements about how I feel may be: I feel angry; I feel excited; I feel depressed. I statements about what I need may be: I need a hug; I need a glass of water; I need some quiet time. I statements about what I think could be: I think I will not go; I think I am lost; I think the team should trade for a good quarterback.

You messages are about someone else. They are your perceptions of how someone else feels, about what someone else needs, and about what someone else thinks. Some examples of you messages regarding someone else's feelings could be: You look angry; You seem excited; You appear depressed. You messages regarding someone's needs could be: You need a hug; You need a glass of water; You need some quiet time. You messages regarding someone's thoughts could be: What do you think about nuclear energy? Do you think the team should trade for a good quarterback?

I Statements and You Messages

I statements make me the center of attention, the star of the moment. I statements focus on me, tell about me, describe me.

You messages make someone else the center of attention, the star of the moment. You messages focus on someone else, tell about someone else, describe someone else. The big difference is that messages about someone else are only guesses or perceptions about how they look, how they feel, and what they need. Only that person knows for sure if the you messages are accurate.

Ownership of Feelings

Another difference between I statements and you messages centers on ownership. When used appropriately, I statements convey ownership of feelings, thoughts, and needs. Each person is responsible for his or her self.

That is, no one can make you feel, think, or need something you don't want. Although others can influence your decision, the final say belongs to you and no one else.

You have the final say about how you feel.

When people use I statements, they are essentially taking ownership of what they feel, think, or need. Taking ownership of your own feelings, thoughts, and needs is the first step in using I statements appropriately.

Ownership of feelings cannot be expressed with you messages simply because no one can own anyone else's feelings, thoughts, and needs. Ownership is a highly individualistic concept.

Appropriate Use of I Statements

I statements are used appropriately when a person wants to send some message about him or herself. As we just mentioned, such statements convey ownership and represent a clear statement of the person's feelings, thoughts, and needs.

- "I am angry with you because you started a fight with Billie."
- "I am not aware of any restaurant open this time of night."
- "I need to spend some time by myself in order to unwind."

Inappropriate Use of I Statements

I statements are often used inappropriately. Sometimes people make I statements in order to manipulate others into doing something. Some examples of the inappropriate use of I statements may be:

- "I am so upset at what you are doing that I might have a heart attack."
- "If you don't do it my way, I will get a migraine headache."

These statements are manipulative. Their intent is to control someone's behavior. The clear message and the ownership of the feeling is not present.

I statements to manipulate are inappropriate.

Appropriate Use of You Messages

You messages are used appropriately in three ways.

To Give Choices

You messages work well in combination with choices and consequences: A message is being sent to the child which describes alternative plans of behavior and their expected consequences.

An example may be:

> "Stephen, you have a choice. You can clean your room now, or you can clean your room later. However, if your room is not cleaned by 6 p.m., you can't watch T.V. tonight. It's your choice."

In this instance, a you message was sent to Stephen, and Stephen was the center of attention. As you already know, giving children choices helps them develop a sense of responsibility.

You messages work well with choices.

To Give Praise

You messages work well when praising someone for being or for doing. When praising, the center of attention naturally belongs to someone else. That's the time for a whole string of you messages.

- "You must feel very proud."
- "You must feel really good."
- "You have done that so well."

Letting someone know how proud you are would be good also, as long as the center of attention remains with the other person.

To Gain Clarification

You messages are ideal to send when clarification is desired. As mentioned earlier, you messages are your perceptions or guesses about how another person feels, what another person is thinking, or what another person needs. When a you message is sent requesting clarification, we are essentially asking for validation. Are my perceptions right or wrong?

Some examples are:

- "You seem to be really angry."
- "You appear sad."
- "You don't seem to like the play."

The receiver is able to respond to the question(s) based on a quick inventory of how he is feeling. Sending a you message for clarification helps the sender know the state of being of the receiver, as well as letting the receiver know how he appears to be acting.

A you message can be sent for clarification.

Inappropriate Use of You Messages

No one likes to have negative or bad feelings. It doesn't feel good to be angry, sad, afraid, depressed, or out of control, although all people have these feelings at some time or another during their lives. When we do have negative feelings, it's often difficult to take full responsibility for the feelings. It's easier and much safer to blame someone else for the way we feel. In that way, we don't have to take responsibility for our actions.

Blaming others for your feelings is inappropriate.

Statements like: "You made me angry;" "You give me a headache;" or "You made me lose control" are good examples of you messages that are blaming. They are the adult version of the child's "He made me do it."

You messages should not be blaming.

Increasing Family Communication

The appropriate use of I statements and you messages is critical to establishing and enhancing communication among family members. The ability to accept and receive praise, to implement nonabusive behavior management strategies, to listen to the needs, feelings, and thoughts of your children, and to communicate your own feelings, thoughts, and needs all center around your success at using I statements and you messages. The time and energy you invest in learning how to send I statements and you messages will pay rich dividends in increasing honest communication between you and your children, mate, and friends.

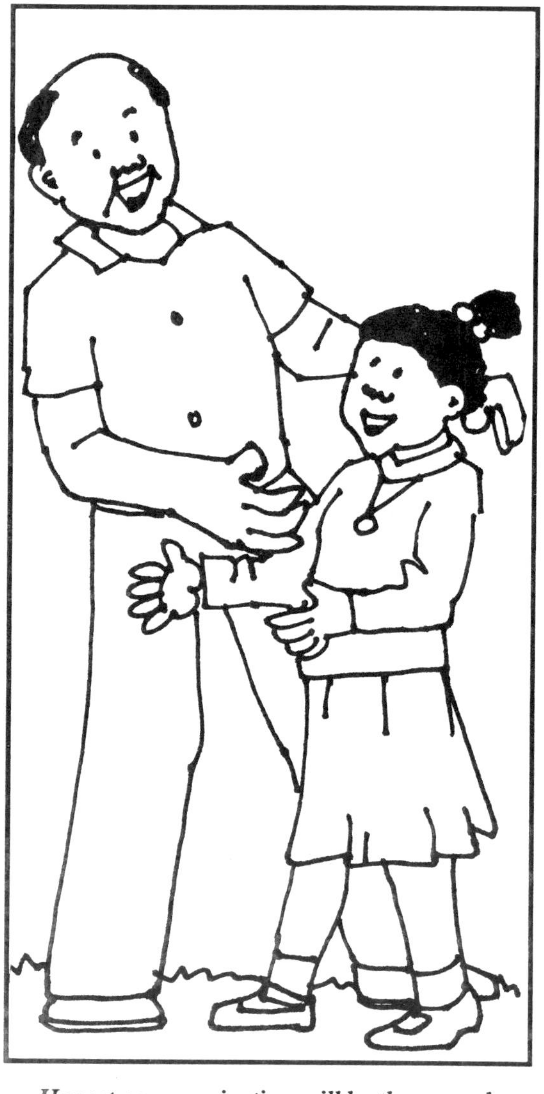

Honest communication will be the reward.

31

Problem Solving and Decision Making

Parents and children are not always going to agree on what things to do, or what to eat, or which clothes to wear, or when to go to bed. Learning how to solve problems that come up between you and your preschooler will result in both of you feeling good.

Problem Solving

Problem solving is what you do when you know you have a problem but don't know what to do.

Decision Making

Decision making is what you do when you know what your alternatives are.

How to Solve Problems and Make Decisions

The following six steps will increase your ability to solve problems and make decisions.

1. **Write down the problem.** Make a full sentence describing the problem.

   - "I don't have enough money."
   - "I don't like the way my house looks."
   - "My relationships aren't good."
   - "I don't feel fulfilled."

"I know I have a problem, what should I do?"

2. **Determine ownership of the problem.** Is your child doing something you don't approve of but does not see the behavior as a problem?

3. **Write the goal statement.** Using the phrase "how to" as a beginning is suggestive and helpful.

   - "How to have enough money."
   - "How to like the way my house looks."
   - "How to have good relationships."
   - "How to make myself feel fulfilled."

   This is the **hardest** step because you have to be very clear about what you want. There is a big difference between having enough money and making more money. You might have enough money if you learn how to live on less and that might make you happier than if you had set making more money as a goal and then had to get another job.

4. **List as many ways as you can to achieve your goal.** Ask friends for ideas and think of other creative ideas. This is an individual brainstorming process and you should let yourself be as wild and funny as you can because it might trigger other ideas or help you to look at your possible solutions in a new way.

5. **Pick out your favorite three ideas.** List the positive and negative payoffs for each one.

6. **Make your decision from one of your ideas.** If a decision isn't clear, go back to the problem statement and the goal statement and make sure they are still what you want to say.

"Now I know what to do!"

Problem Solving and Decision Making Worksheet

1. Problem Statement: ______________________________

____

2. Whose problem is it? ______________________________

3. Write down goal statement – what do you want to see instead? ______________________________

____

4. List ways to achieve the goal statement:

   a. ______________________________

   b. ______________________________

   c. ______________________________

   d. ______________________________

   e. ______________________________

   f. ______________________________

5. List the positive and negative payoffs for top three goals:

Positives	Negatives
a.	a.
b.	b.
c.	c.

6. If the decision isn't clear from the list, go back to the problem statement and the goal statement and make sure they still are what you want to say.

32

Helping Children With Feelings

Feelings are the way we see ourselves and others. Feelings are our reaction to the world around us. Each of us is our feelings more than we are our thoughts. Helping children express and handle their feelings lets them know the way they view others and the world is important.

Learn the steps in helping children express their feelings.

1. **Label what you see or think you see.** If you don't see anything, guess and describe the feeling the child might have.

   - "You look really angry."
   - "You look so proud. Did something good happen?"
   - "I heard your friend is moving. You must feel really bad about that."

"You look disappointed. What happened?"

2. **Don't hog the conversation. Let the child do the talking.** It's hard for a child to follow his or her own train of thought if someone is interrupting or blaming or giving advice, etc. Simply look interested in what the child is saying and listen.

Let the child do the talking.

3. **When your child wants something, honor the desire.** If you're in the grocery store and the child wants a toy, instead of just saying "NO!" try,

   "If I could, I'd buy you every toy in this store."

   Or if the child wants cookies or candy, try,

   "If I could, I'd buy you not only those but also another kind for after dinner and still another kind for before bed and three different kinds for breakfast. Then, if you weren't sick, I'd buy you 29 more kinds all for you." Name the child's favorite kinds in the beginning part. This helps children understand that you value their desires, that you want them to be happy, and it doesn't always keep you in the position of saying "no, no, no."

33

Improving Specific Self-Esteem

Our self-esteem is the way we feel about ourselves. When we feel good about ourselves, we treat others the same way. Building a positive self-esteem in ourselves and in our children can be accomplished through using positive, not negative labels to refer to ourselves and our children.

Improving Specific Self-Esteem

1. Write down your children's names and positive/negative labels.

Child's Name	Positive Label	Negative Label
a. ________	a. ________	a. ________
b. ________	b. ________	b. ________
c. ________	c. ________	c. ________
d. ________	d. ________	d. ________
e. ________	e. ________	e. ________

2. Suggestions on how to help children develop a positive label.

a. ______________________________

b. ______________________________

c. ______________________________

d. ______________________________

e. ______________________________

f. ______________________________

g. ______________________________

h. ______________________________

i. ______________________________

Improving Specific Self-Esteem (Continued)

3. Write down three specific ways you can help to improve your child's self-esteem.

   a. ____________________

   b. ____________________

   c. ____________________

4. Write down a negative label and a positive label you have for **yourself.**

Negative Label for Self	**Positive Label for Self**
____________	____________

5. Three things I can do to improve my own self-esteem.

   a. ____________________

   b. ____________________

   c. ____________________

34

Stimulate and Communicate

Talking to and touching your baby are two important things to do to help your child develop a good attitude about him or herself and about life in general. Let's examine why and how talking to and touching your child is important.

Talking to Your Child

Children are born with the capacity to understand words and to learn to talk. In fact, children start to communicate their needs from the moment they are born; they just don't start using words until a couple of years later. When a baby hears his mother's voice, he will stop what he is doing and will listen. When a child is almost four months old, when someone talks to him, he will respond with noises. The noises won't be words, but nevertheless, your baby is communicating.

Children communicate their needs.

Baby's First Sounds

The first sounds babies will make are sounds like **e's** and **eh's** and **a's**. Babies make these sounds when they need something. They are called "discomfort sounds." Another name for discomfort sounds is crying. Children will cry in sounds of **e**, **eh**, and **a**.

Soon babies learn other sounds like **ah**, **oh**, **oo**. These sounds are called "comfort sounds" and you'll usually hear them when the baby feels content.

When you pay attention to the different sounds of comfort and discomfort, you are helping establish a way your baby can talk to you. The child learns that when he makes these noises, his mother will respond by doing something. These noises will begin to show up in combinations around six months of age. At this point, the baby will start to babble.

Reinforcing Baby's Sounds

Sometimes your baby will say something that sounds like a word, but isn't. Smile and praise your child for saying that noise. That's baby talk. Imitate that noise and say it back to him. When you imitate his sounds, he'll probably say them right back. Enjoy those sounds and give your child a hug. Tell him how pleased you are that he is talking.

Praise and imitate the noises your child makes.

Language Development

Talk to your children all the time. When you're feeding them, changing their diapers, giving them a bath, putting them to bed, talk to them so they can learn to put words to certain actions and objects. We call this language development and it's very important for helping children express their needs in words. To help stimulate language development, read books with your children. Anytime during the day is a good time to read stories together, but it's an especially nice thing to do before children go to sleep.

Talk to your children.

Describing how children feel is another excellent time to help children develop their language. Use words to describe how you think your children are feeling: "Adam seems very sad right now," or "Tami is feeling happy." Putting words to feelings will help children be able to express how they are feeling—a skill you certainly want to develop.

Stimulating Your Child

You already are probably aware that young children are explorers in diapers. They love to touch and nothing is sacred. If it's in reach, the child will touch, grab, twist, bite, or pull on it. Of course you do want to baby proof your house to reduce the risk of injury to your child by putting unsafe objects and chemicals out of his reach. Give your child safe things to touch and play with.

Stimulating your child is very important to his overall development. We have listed several things you can do to help stimulate your child.

- Give your child safe things to touch of different textures: hard, soft, fuzzy, sticky, creamy, etc.

Let your child touch safe, different things.

- Let your child play with objects of different colors and sizes.

- Have colored shapes, pictures of animals, and books nearby the changing table so when your child gets bored with having his diaper changed, he can look at pictures instead.

- Hang mobiles by the changing table or above his bed. Make sure they are the kind your baby can see when he is laying down looking up. Also, make sure the mobiles are not accessible for your baby to pull himself up, or get tangled up in.

- Dance with and sing to your baby. Babies love gentle rhythmic movements.

Sing and dance with your child.

- Stimulate your child's awareness of his body by giving him a massage. You know how nice massages feel.

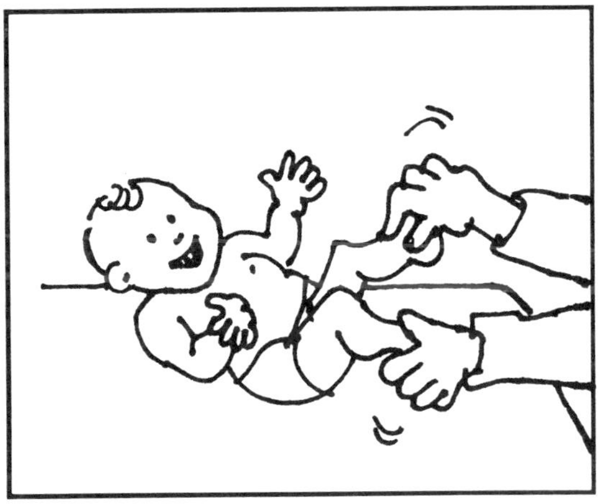

Massages feel good for children also.

These are some simple suggestions for talking and stimulating your child. A conscious effort on your part will encourage your child to find life exciting and wonderful.

35

Toilet Training

Teaching children to use the toilet is not as hard as perhaps you are imagining. With careful planning and the right conditions, children can learn to use the toilet in a matter of a few days to a few weeks. But before you start to teach your child how to use the toilet, there are many important things that must be checked first.

Is Your Child Ready?

Age

Don't bother to begin teaching your child how to use the toilet if he is not at least two years old or older. Many children are trained when they are around two years old. If you plan on starting before two years of age, you will create undo amounts of anxiety in you and your child. This anxiety is likely to lead your child to feelings of failure and a low self-concept.

Muscle Control

Can your child walk yet? Can he put little objects into bigger objects? Does he have good muscle control? If he doesn't, he won't be able to control his bladder or bowels. Physical coordination is necessary before you begin toilet teaching.

Physical Development

The maturity of the bladder is also important to consider. A couple of indicators that suggest your child's bladder capacity is ready for toilet training: a dry diaper after napping, and a steady flow of urine rather than several episodes of dribbles.

Communication

Your child will need to be able to communicate his intentions to urinate or have a bowel movement before he can be taught to successfully use the potty. He has to be able to make some sound or make some facial expression or physical movement to let you know he has to go. If he cannot communicate his intentions, he's not ready to learn to use the potty.

Your child must be able to communicate.

Follow Verbal Instructions

Your child will have to be able to follow instructions before you can start successful toilet teaching. Simply, if a child can't follow verbal directions, when you tell him to "hurry and go use the potty," he may be thinking you are talking some foreign language. Give your child verbal instructions and see if he can follow through. If he can't, successful toilet teaching will not be accomplished.

Being able to follow verbal instruction is a must.

Desire

Lastly, before you begin toilet teaching, you have to determine whether or not your child has the desire to learn. All the other preconditions listed will serve little value if your child simply refuses to use the potty. Desire to use the potty will speed up the learning process greatly.

Your child has to have the desire.

Before You Begin Your Teaching

The following suggestions will help you prepare your child to use the potty.

Words to Use

Parents need to help children decide on words to use to indicate that the child needs to either urinate or have a bowel movement. Use any words you like, but it helps if the words make sense so others can understand about your child's needs when you're not around. Some words parents use are silly, confusing, and eventually embarrassing. Words like tinkle, shimkle, udo, shooo-shooo, wee wee, tee tee, #1 or #2, kaka, or BM all mean the child has to urinate or have a bowel movement. The words the child will use depends a great deal on the preference of the parents. Keep the words simple so a child can say them, yet understandable enough for others.

Model the Appropriate Behavior

Let the child see you and other family members using the bathroom. When you go, you can say "Mommy (Daddy) is going pee pee in the toilet." That way your daughter or son notices how adults use the toilet. The same sex parent as child is generally preferable. Children may become confused watching opposite sex family members urinate. If you're a bit embarrassed by the thought of your child watching you go to the bathroom, ask an older son or daughter. Older siblings generally don't mind going to the bathroom with their younger brother or sister around.

Model the appropriate behavior.

Buy a Potty Chair

Before you begin teaching your child how to use the toilet, it's a great idea to first purchase a potty chair. Purchasing a potty chair encourages your child to see it, play with it, and become familiar with it before he begins to use it.

The separate unit potty chair, the one that stands on the floor, is generally considered better than the unit that attaches to the toilet. The separate standing unit allows the child to place his/her feet on the floor which adds to feelings of security and comfort.

Potty chairs that sit on the floor are best.

Let the child examine the potty, play with it, take it apart, carry it around, before he begins to use it. Again, the more comfortable the child is with the potty, the greater the chance that he/she will want to use it.

Buy Training Pants

Your child will need to wear training pants instead of diapers when you begin toilet teaching. Help him learn to pull them up and pull them down. Fancy looking training pants with pictures of your child's favorite singer, or cartoon character, might make it just a bit more enjoyable to wear training pants. If your child is still in diapers, do not attempt to start toilet training. There will be just too much frustration in getting the diaper off in time to use the potty.

In Starting the Training

When you decide your child is ready to learn how to use the potty, try to pick a good day to begin.

It probably will help both you and your child to begin the task of learning to use the toilet if both of you are in good moods. A cranky child, or one who has had a bad night's sleep, can make the task of toilet teaching very frustrating. In this situation, the parents who desire to teach the child may also become frustrated and unknowingly non-supportive and even punitive. Teaching your child to use the potty should be fun, not confrontive.

Pick a day when both of you are in good moods.

Plan to set aside the entire day for helping and supporting your child. Make the task of introducing the potty your only task for the day.

Teaching Potty Training

1. **Try to make a realistic guess when your child will likely need to use the potty.** After lunch, before nap, after nap, after breakfast? Becoming aware helps you to be available and pay extra special notice to possible potty times.

Be aware of possible potty times.

2. **When you notice your child is about to urinate or have a bowel movement, help him pull his pants down, and guide him to the potty.**

3. **Talk to your child.** Use the words you decided on for urination and bowel movement. Say to your child, "Adam is about ready to make poo poo in his potty. Oh, what an exciting time."

4. **Stay with your child in the bathroom while he is having a bowel movement.** Keep him company, read a story or two.

5. **Praise his efforts.** It might take some children a while to do their bowel movement. Don't pressure your child, support him.

6. **When he is finished, praise your child.** Don't be afraid to let him know how proud you are of his efforts, not of him. Children are anxious to get their parents' attention and approval. Don't be stingy with your praise.

Praise your child for his efforts when he is done.

7. **Teach your child how to wipe himself.** Girls should always be taught to wipe themselves from front to back. It's a good habit to start early, one that will help prevent bladder infections in the future.

8. **After your child has gone in the potty, you can empty the potty in several ways:**

- You can empty the potty in the toilet and flush the toilet while your child watches.
- Your child can help you empty the potty perhaps by flushing the toilet.
- You can empty the potty after your child has left the room.

Some children are very sensitive and may become upset that a product of their body is disappearing. Consequently, you may not want to flush the toilet until they leave the room. Other children are less worried about that issue and may want to take an active role in discarding the potty material. Be sensitive to your child's needs and act accordingly.

Be sensitive to your child's needs.

Accidents Will Happen

Expect that your child will have accidents in the beginning. Accidents are a normal occurrence. When an accident happens, talk to your child and reassure him. "Oh Oh. Adam made poo poo in his pants. Too bad. Next time Adam will do poo poo in the potty. Let's change your pants. Poo poo in your pants probably doesn't feel very good." The main thing to remember when accidents happen: **Do Not Make a Big Deal About Them.** Make a big deal when your child uses the potty.

If your child misses the potty and wets or soils the floor, reassuringly tell him, "Oh Adam missed the potty this time. Can you put your pee pee or poo poo in the potty next time? Thanks for trying son!" Always encourage your child to use the potty.

Expect accidents in the beginning.

If your child begins to act as if he never heard of, let alone used a potty, remain supportive and talk to your child. Several things may be going on that could be contributing to your child's regressing:

- The child feels less attention is being paid to him.
- A new brother or sister in the family has taken over the spotlight.
- Too much pressure is being put on using the potty correctly.
- Family problems, separations, divorces, extended absences, moving to a new home, illness, etc.

If your child continues to wet and soil himself, put him back in diapers. This way the pressure is lessened for you and for him.

Putting diapers on will lessen the pressure.

Some Final Points to Remember

- **Never, ever use punishment in teaching your child to use the potty.** Punitive, abusive practices only cause increased anxiety and can lead to very severe problems. The point that punishment is harmful in teaching children to use the potty cannot be stressed enough.

Do not use punishment in your teaching!

- **Once your child has begun to use the potty, keep the potty in the bathroom.** Don't get into the habit of moving the potty in front of the TV to amuse your child. You don't move your toilet in front of the TV, so don't move the potty. The bathroom is the place where toilets and potties belong.

Keep your child's potty in the bathroom.

- **Children are constantly learning who they are and what values they have from the important people in their lives.** Parents are probably the most important of all the people children interact with. Teaching your child to use the toilet is an important time between both of you. Through your teaching and support, help your child realize that he or she is a winner: someone you are proud of, someone you enjoy being with, someone who tries real hard.

The greatest single outcome that a child can learn from the whole experience of toilet teaching is positive regard for himself or herself as a boy or girl. Keep this fact in mind as you're helping your child learn to use the potty.

Being potty trained is a good feeling!

36

Verbal Management

Helping children learn to behave appropriately can be partly accomplished by the messages we give them when they act inappropriately.

Verbal Management

Utilizing verbal management requires you to be aware of six easy steps. Review the following steps and examples to learn the techniques of verbal management.

1. **Express your feelings strongly.**

   - "Janet, I am very upset that you are running around the grocery store behaving like a wild woman."
   - "Billy, I am furious that you left my scissors in your little brother's room."

2. **Tell your child very clearly what you expect.**

   - "I expect you to walk and talk quietly when we are in the grocery store."
   - "I expect you to return my scissors after you use them."

3. **Show your child how to be helpful or if it's too late for that, how to make amends.**

   - "Janet, you could help me by getting a box of your favorite cereal from that shelf over there."
   - "Billy, you can scrub those scissors until every bit of paste is off them, and then you can dry them well so they won't rust."

Show your child how to be helpful.

4. **Give your child a choice as we learned in choices and consequences.**

   - "Janet, you can either help me by getting the cereal, or you can sit in the grocery cart." Then if she doesn't help, put her in the cart and say, "I see you have decided to sit in the cart."
   - "Billy, you can either return my scissors when you are finished with them, or you can leave them alone."

5. **Take action, DO SOMETHING!**

   - Leave Janet home next time. When she howls in protest, tell her she cannot go this time because she didn't behave last time.
   - Lock up the scissors. When Billy howls, say, "Yes, until you can return the scissors after you use them, I am going to keep my scissors where I can find them."

Take action; do something.

6. **Problem solve. With your child, try to decide what to do next time. First of all, state a goal for both of you to agree on.**

   - Janet will not run and yell in the grocery store next time.
   - Billy will put back the scissors after he uses them.

When you are both quiet and calm, talk with your child about the goal. For instance, "Janet, how can we make sure you behave well in the store?" Janet will have some suggestions, you will have some suggestions, so make a list of **all** suggestions just like in brainstorming. Then talk about them with her to decide which ones you and she like or don't like.

Janet's Suggestions:

Let me run and be wild.

Hit me when I yell.

Give me candy so I am happy in the store.

Let me watch TV when I get home if I am good.

Take a friend for me to play with.

Let me read a book in the car if I am not good.

Janet's Suggestions

Mom's Suggestions:

You stay home if you don't behave.

I'll buy you fruit to eat in the store.

We'll go after nap so you aren't tired.

I'll drop you off at Granny's house.

You get to choose two things to buy if you are good.

We will read a book together afterwards.

Mom's Suggestions

Together you both cross out the ones you don't like. You can say, "I don't want to hit you. I don't like that idea." Janet can say, "I don't want to go to Granny's while you go to the store." So you cross both of these suggestions off the list. Then together choose a problem solution you both like.

Find a solution you both agree on.

37

Behavior Management Review Sheet

Helping children manage their behavior is a combination of knowing which techniques to use and when to use them. The Nurturing Program promotes effective behavior management strategies designed to help children gain mastery of their behavior. Coupled with an empathic awareness of children's needs, these techniques will promote healthier parent/child interactions.

Behavior Management Review Sheet

TASK	PROGRESS		
	Doing Well	Need a Little More Work	Need a Lot More Work
1. Behavior Management			
2. Family Rules			
3. Praise			
4. Time-Out			
5. Choices & Consequences			
6. I Statements/You Messages			
7. Criticism, Confrontation			
8. Verbal Management			
9. Ignoring			
10. Problem Solving			
11. Redirection			

38

Families and Chemical Use Questionnaire

Chemical use becomes a problem in most families when it becomes excessive. When parents use chemicals, they model for their children one way to cope, or to relax, or to have fun. Excessive use of any chemical is not a healthy model for children to learn. Complete the following questionnaire and learn about your chemical use.

Families And Chemical Use Questionnaire

The following questions are designed to only increase your awareness about your chemical use and the chemical use of any family member. The word "chemical" in these questions refers to all mood altering substances such as alcohol, pot, speed, uppers, downers, etc. Answer the questions as honestly as you can. You will not be required to turn this questionnaire in to anyone.

About You	**Yes**	**No**
1. Do you feel you have a chemical use (pot, alcohol, speed, downers, uppers, etc.) problem?	______	______
2. Do you often use a chemical to feel better?	______	______
3. Do you often use a chemical to "get through the day?"	______	______
4. Do you spend more money on your chemical than you planned?	______	______
5. Do you feel annoyed or irritated if your family or friends discuss your chemical use?	______	______
6. Have you had any arguments with your family or friends because of your chemical use?	______	______
7. Have you ever failed to keep a promise you made to yourself about cutting down on your chemical use?	______	______
8. Do you tend to use your chemical at times when you feel angry, disappointed, depressed, anxious, or lonely?	______	______
9. Have you ever been careless of your family's welfare when you've been using a chemical? (Driving under the influence, falling asleep with a burning cigarette, not caring where your kids were, blowing a paycheck on chemicals, hitting a family member when under the influence?)	______	______
10. Do you use chemicals in the morning to help you recover from the night before?	______	______

About Your Family		
1. Do you feel a member of your family has a chemical use problem?	______	______
2. Do you lie awake worrying about your family member (of whatever age)?	______	______
3. Do you feel frustrated in your attempts to control your family member?	______	______
4. Do you argue with your family member about his or her use of chemicals?	______	______
5. Do you find it increasingly difficult to communicate with your family member?	______	______
6. Do you find yourself lying or covering up for your family member?	______	______
7. Do you feel resentful or hostile toward your family member?	______	______
8. Do you worry about your family member's behavior affecting other members of the family?	______	______
9. Has the family member been confronted about his/her use of chemicals?	______	______
10. Has the family member denied his/her use of chemicals?	______	______

39

Emergency Parenting and Survival Kits

Not losing sight of your own needs is critical to remaining a nurturing parent. The following emergency parenting and survival kit should be completed and referred to when times get tough.

Emergency Parenting Kit

1. Write down five things to do when times are tough being a parent.

   a.______________________________

   b.______________________________

   c.______________________________

   d.______________________________

   e.______________________________

2. Write down ten things to do when times get tough being a parent.

   a.______________________________

   b.______________________________

   c.______________________________

   d.______________________________

   e.______________________________

   f.______________________________

   g.______________________________

   h.______________________________

   i.______________________________

   j.______________________________

3. When times get tough, start with the first suggestion and go down the list.

Emergency Survival Kit

1. Write down five things to do to make yourself feel better when you are feeling down.

   a.____________________

   b.____________________

   c.____________________

   d.____________________

   e.____________________

2. Write down ten things to do when you are feeling down.

   a.____________________

   b.____________________

   c.____________________

   d.____________________

   e.____________________

   f.____________________

   g.____________________

   h.____________________

   i.____________________

   j.____________________

3. When times get tough, start with the first suggestion and go down the list.

40

Home Practice Exercises

Home Practice Exercises

Following are Home Practice Exercises for you to complete. They will help you practice the new skills you learned during each session. Write your responses on a separate sheet of paper. Do your best and share your responses with your home visitor during the next session. (Sessions 2, 44, and 45 do not have Practice Exercises.)

Activities Manual Session	Parent Handbook Location

Session 1 Orientation — **Section 1**

a. List the ways you currently manage your children's behavior. What punishments and rewards do you use?
b. Which of these techniques do you like; which don't you like?
c. What do you think you would like to learn instead to manage your children's behavior?
d. Complete family log.

Session 3 Discipline and Punishment — **Section 2**

a. List ways you currently manage your children's behavior. What punishments and rewards do you use?
b. Which of these techniques do you like; which don't you like?
c. Complete family log.

Session 4 Family Rules — **Section 3**

a. Review the proposed list of rules with other family members to get their input.
b. Make appropriate changes in rules, rewards, and consequences.
c. Be prepared to implement the rules by the next session.
d. Complete family log.

Session 5 Personal Needs and Payoffs to Behavior — **Section 4**

a. Do at least one thing to meet a need of your own. How did you feel?
b. Do at least one thing to meet a need of your children. How do you think your children felt?
c. Complete family log.

Session 6 Spoiling Your Children — **Section 5**

a. Attempt reducing the spoiled, unacceptable behavior of the child by practicing the suggestions presented in the earlier activity. Follow the recommendations offered.
b. Complete family log.

Session 7 Personal Power — **Section 6**

a. Practice using positive control to manage behavior.
b. Practice using your personal power to enhance self-esteem.
c. Provide children an opportunity to use their personal power to take responsibility for their behavior.
d. Praise yourself and your children for being and doing at least twice.
e. Complete family log.

Activities Manual Session	Parent Handbook Location
Session 8 Praise for Being and Doing	**Section 7**

a. Praise each child twice: once for being, once for doing.
b. Praise yourself twice for either being or doing.
c. Complete family log.

Session 9 Red, White, and Bruises	**Section 8**

a. Identify two times during the week when you felt like hitting your children but didn't.
b. Identify what you did instead of hitting.
c. Identify instances when the family rules seemed to be working or not working.
d. Complete family log.

Session 10 Hurting Touch	**Section 8**

a. Find a chance to talk to other family members about hurting touch. See what they remember of the experiences. Other family members can include children, husbands/wives, grandparents, siblings, parents, etc.
b. Complete family log.

Session 11 Baby Proofing	**Section 9**

a. Use the baby proof checklist to modify your house environment, making the house safe for your child.
b. Complete family log.

Session 12 Verbal and Physical Redirection	**Section 10**

a. Practice verbal and physical redirection at least five times.
b. Praise your child for cooperating.
c. Complete family log.

Session 13 Touch and Talk	**Section 11**

a. Practice touching yourself in a nurturing way.
b. Practice touching and talking to your children in a nurturing way.
c. Complete family log.

Session 14 Time-Out	**Section 12**

a. Use time-out at least twice when rules are broken.
b. Praise child two times; self one time.
c. Do one thing to reinforce your positive feelings of self.
d. Complete family log.

Session 15 Ages and Stages	**Sections 13, 14, 15, 16**

a. Review the information on development.
b. Note at least one thing you learned which you didn't know before about each of your children.
c. Praise yourself and your children.
d. Complete family log.

Activities Manual Session	Parent Handbook Location

Session 16 Skill Strips — **Section 17**

a. Pay close attention to the skills and abilities of your child(ren). Note one thing that you observe that you weren't aware of before.
b. Upon task accomplishment or effort, praise your child for doing.
c. Tonight, praise your child for doing.
d. Complete family log.

Session 17 Troublesome Feelings — **Sections 18, 19**

a. Deal with troublesome feelings with new awareness.
b. Be aware of misery-making beliefs when they arise and think of better choices.
c. Complete family log.

Session 18 Handling Stress — **Section 20**

a. Write down the number of times you felt stress, what caused the stress, and how you handled it.
b. Practice handling stress with one of the new techniques learned.
c. Complete family log.

Session 19 Nurturing Diapering and Dressing Routines — **Sections 21, 22**

a. Practice implementing the nurturing diapering and dressing routine with each of your children.
b. Complete family log.

Session 20 Nurturing Feeding Time Routines — **Section 23**

a. Practice implementing the nurturing feeding routine with each of your children.
b. Continue implementing the nurturing routine during diapering and dressing.
c. Complete family log.

Session 21 Nutrition and Dinnertime — **Section 23**

a. Do one thing to make family dinnertime nicer.
b. Serve a nutritious snack.
c. Practice Nurturing Routines.
d. Complete family log.

Session 22 Nurturing Bath Time Routines — **Section 24**

a. Practice implementing the nurturing bath time routine with each of your children.
b. Continue to practice the other nurturing routines during feeding times, and diapering and dressing times.
c. Complete family log.

Session 23 Nurturing Bed Time Routines — **Section 25**

a. Practice implementing the nurturing bedtime routine with each of your children.
b. Continue to practice the other nurturing routines during feeding times, diapering and dressing times, and bath times.
c. Complete family log.

Activities Manual Session	Parent Handbook Location
Session 24 Anger	**Sections 26, 27**

a. Practice handling anger by using one of the three alternatives identified.
b. Pay attention to the times you get angry and to the issue related to your anger. Is there a pattern? Are certain needs you have not being given a chance for fulfillment?
c. Complete family log.

Session 25 Choices and Consequences — **Section 28**

a. Use choices and consequences at least three times.
b. Praise child(ren) twice and self once.
c. Continue to use time-out for misbehavior.
d. Complete family log.

Session 26 Ignoring — **Section 29**

a. Practice ignoring twice.
b. Praise desirable behavior.
c. Complete family log.

Session 27 Personal Space

a. Notice two times your personal space had been violated.
b. Notice one time your child(ren)'s personal space was violated.
c. Notice one time you could have violated your child(ren)'s personal space but didn't.
d. Complete family log.

Session 28 Our Bodies

a. During diapering or bath times, refer to body parts using correct terminology.
b. Complete family log.

Session 29 Scary Touch

a. Review with all your children the concepts of scary touch, body part terminology, ownership of body, and permission to touch.
b. Complete family log.

Session 30 Body Map

a. Practice positive touch with something – enjoy touching something.
b. Practice positive touch with someone – enjoy touching someone. (Remember you are a person.)
c. Touch your child(ren) in a nurturing way.
d. Complete family log.

Session 31 Criticism & Confrontation

a. Practice confrontation twice.
b. Complete family log.

Activities Manual Session	Parent Handbook Location
Session 32 I Statements and You Messages	**Section 30**

a. Identify ownership in problem situations.
b. Make three I statements.
c. Make three you messages.
d. Complete family log.

Session 33 Problem Solving and Decision Making	**Section 31**

a. Help your child learn to problem solve.
b. Solve a problem, make a decision (your own or family's).
c. Praise each of your children twice: once for being, once for doing.
d. Complete family log.

Session 34 Helping Children with Feelings	**Section 32**

a. Help your child handle a feeling.
b. Praise your child for handling/trying to handle the feeling.
c. Complete family log.

Session 35 Improving Specific Self-Esteem	**Section 33**

a. Do two things to improve your child's self-esteem and self-concept.
b. Do two things to improve your own self-esteem and self-concept.
c. Complete family log.

Session 36 Stimulating and Communicating	**Section 34**

a. Do one activity with your child that is stimulating.
b. Practice talking to your child by describing his/her feelings during feeding time, bath time, and changing time.
c. Pay attention to your child's ways of communicating to you.
d. Complete family log.

Session 37 Toilet Training	**Section 35**

a. Practice potty training your child with the techniques and steps identified in the resource material.
b. Complete family log.

Session 38 Verbal Management	**Section 36**

a. Use verbal management at least once.
b. Model self praise: praise self out loud in front of child.
c. Try the problem solving techniques.
d. Complete family log.

Session 39 Self-Expression	

a. Have one playtime activity per child that encourages self-expression and creativity.
b. Complete family log.

Session 40 People and Possessions

a. Notice someone treating another person as a possession.
b. Notice yourself treating or about to treat someone as a possession.
c. Notice someone treating or about to treat you as a possession.
d. Complete family log.

Session 41 Review of Behavior Management — Section 37

a. Practice the techniques in behavior management identified as "Need a Little More Work" and "Need a Lot More Work."
b. Complete family log.

Session 42 Positive Self-Talk

a. Notice a time when you start becoming overly critical of yourself.
b. Practice using positive self-talk at times when you begin being self-critical.
c. Complete family log.

Session 43 Families and Chemical Use — Section 38

a. Identify how you are feeling just prior to and after taking a chemical of choice (aspirin, alcohol, pot, speed, sedatives, etc.)
b. Identify all the types of chemicals that are used regularly by family members during the week.
c. Complete family log.